US POLITICS
ANNUAL UPDATE
2025

Anthony J. Bennett
Simon Lemieux

US Politics Annual Update 2025

Anthony J. Bennett
Simon Lemieux

ISBN 9781917109383

A CIP catalogue record for this book
is available from the British Library

Published 2024

Tricorn Books,
Treadgolds
1a Bishop Street
Portsmouth
PO1 3HN

TRICORN
BOOKS

US POLITICS
ANNUAL UPDATE
2025

CONTENTS

PREFACE

The *US Politics Annual Update* is back! I started this publication as a young teacher at the Royal Hospital School, Ipswich, back in 1982. In 2003, it was taken up by Philip Allan, a small educational publisher in Oxfordshire. Five years later, Philip Allan became part of the Hodder Education empire who published it until 2023. Now, after a short break, I've teamed up with Simon Lemieux to relaunch what has for many years been the *Hodder US Politics Annual Update*. We're grateful to Jenny Reynolds and Will Goodfellow at Hodder Education for facilitating the handover. Our aim is to publish annually through Tricorn Books.

Simon and I are the lead authors of the two main Hodder A-level US politics textbooks – Simon leads the team on the AQA book and I lead on the Edexcel book. Between us we've got decades of experience teaching American politics and acting as A-level examiners so we know what teachers and students of US politics are looking for. Simon hosts a number of conferences for teachers and students of US politics through the year. He's also part of the editorial team of *Politics Review*.

Our aim is to update our textbooks each year by surveying what's been happening in US politics over the previous year – in elections, political parties, interest groups, Congress, the Presidency and the Supreme Court. As the past year has been dominated by the presidential election, this year's *Update* is very much focused on that. It will give added insights and detail that students can use to deepen their understanding of US politics and sharpen their essays and exam scripts. There are questions at the back that students might like to use to assist note-making. Having said that, you might have bought this book, not as an A-level teacher or student, but just as an interested observer of US politics. We trust you, too, will enjoy the story we've told.

Finally, our sincere thanks to Dan and Gail at Tricorn Books for all their hard work and help to bring this venture to print.

Anthony J. Bennett and Simon Lemieux
December 2024

CHAPTER 1

STILL THE INVISIBLE PRIMARY?

What you need to know

- The invisible primary is the term used to refer to the events in the year prior to a presidential election, before the actual primaries and caucuses begin.
- It is called 'invisible' because, traditionally, events that occurred during this period could not actually be seen. They occurred, as it were, mostly behind the scenes, out of the eye of the media.
- The important things that a would-be candidate needs to concentrate on during this period are increasing name recognition (if not nationally known), raising money and putting together the necessary state-based organisation.
- The media plays an important role during this period by staging intra-party televised debates between the would-be candidates.
- The candidate leading in opinion polls at the end of the invisible primary often goes on to become that party's presidential nominee thus enhancing the importance of the invisible primary.
- The term 'invisible primary' first came to prominence as the title of a book by Arthur Hadley, published in 1976.

In 2024, Donald Trump wanted to become the Republican Party's answer to Grover Cleveland. President Cleveland was to date the only president to serve two non-consecutive terms of office. Cleveland was first elected in 1884, but in 1888 was defeated for re-election by Republican Benjamin Harrison. So, four years later, there was a rematch in which Cleveland got his revenge and returned to the White House for his second term. Could Trump do likewise? The fact that, at the time, the Democrats had an incumbent president running for re-election and the Republicans' front-runner was a former incumbent president would mean that the period we call 'the invisible primary' – the calendar year before the first presidential primary is held – would be far less interesting and significant than in most presidential election cycles. Let's consider each party in turn.

The Democrats

Incumbent presidents hoping to win a second term need to avoid any significant internal opponents in their own primaries. Table 1.1 shows the previous eight incumbent presidents who sought re-election between 1976 and 2020. All three presidents who faced significant opposition from within their own parties – Ford (1976), Carter (1980) and Bush (1992) – went down to defeat the following November. But four of the five presidents who faced no significant internal opposition went on to win in November, the only exception being Trump in 2020.

Table 1.1 Incumbent presidents seeking re-election, 1976–2020

President	Party	Year	Any significant intra-party opposition?	Re-elected?
Gerald Ford	R	1976	Yes	No
Jimmy Carter	D	1980	Yes	No
Ronald Reagan	R	1984	No	Yes
George H.W. Bush	R	1992	Yes	No
Bill Clinton	D	1996	No	Yes
George W. Bush	R	2004	No	Yes
Barack Obama	D	2012	No	Yes
Donald Trump	R	2020	No	No

So, the first big question going into the 2024 presidential election cycle was, 'Could President Biden avoid any serious opposition in the primaries?' The short answer was 'yes'. But there are three people we need to mention briefly namely:

- Marianne Williamson – author, philanthropist, political activist
- Dean Phillips – US Representative from Minnesota (2019–25)
- Robert F. Kennedy – environmental lawyer, conspiracy theorist

Of these three, the one who was thought to hold the biggest potential threat to President Biden was Robert Kennedy being a son of Senator Robert F. Kennedy (1925–68) and a nephew of both President John F. Kennedy (1917–63) and Senator Ted Kennedy (1932–2009). But recently, Kennedy had gained notoriety for both his anti-vaccine advocacy and his conspiracy theories regarding Covid-19. His family were so alarmed by his candidacy that they publicly came out in support of President Biden. In October 2023, Kennedy withdrew from the Democratic race and announced he would contest the 2024 presidential election as an independent candidate. Neither Williamson nor Phillips – both of whom battled their way through many of the Democratic primaries – had significant enough name recognition or political standing to pose a serious threat to the President as we shall see in Chapter 2.

Of far more interest during this period of the invisible primary was what was really 'hidden' – going on in the backrooms of the Democratic National Committee (DNC) headquarters in Washington DC. After every presidential election cycle for the past 40 years, the Democrats had set up a working group to see what changes needed to be made to the process for choosing their presidential candidate. Most had passed almost unnoticed. Some had tinkered with the system. But this time round, change – significant change – was on the agenda (see Box 1.1).

Box 1.1 Main provisions of the DNC's Rules and Bylaws Committee, 2023

- Iowa no longer to hold the first-in-the-nation caucuses
- New Hampshire no longer to hold the first-in-the-nation primary
- South Carolina to hold first-in-the-nation primary
- Followed by New Hampshire and Nevada, Georgia and Michigan
- No other states to schedule their contests until March

What had goaded the Democrats into action? Mainly two factors. First, that Iowa and New Hampshire – which for over five decades had staged the opening contests of the presidential candidate selection calendar – are demographically unrepresentative of the nation as a whole (see Table 1.2). They are both relatively small, predominantly white, and mainly rural states. Second, there was the fiasco over the 2020 Iowa Democratic caucuses in which it took three weeks to declare the correct results. The original results even announced the wrong winner! That was the last straw for the Iowa caucuses as far as the Democrats were concerned. They were determined not to have a repeat this time round.

Table 1.2 Demographic characteristics of Iowa and New Hampshire

	Population rank	White	Black	Hispanic
Iowa	30th	86%	5%	7%
New Hampshire	42nd	88%	1%	3%
United States		*61%*	*12%*	*19%*

The states chosen to start the Democratic primaries – South Carolina, Nevada, Georgia and Michigan – were far more representative of the nation as a whole. Neither did it go unnoticed that South Carolina, which was given the prime slot, had been the state that had resurrected the political fortunes of Joe Biden in 2020. Here was their reward. Democrat politicians from Michigan and Georgia clearly approved (see Box 1.2). The DNC didn't get all it wanted. In some states, such as Georgia, Republican-controlled state legislatures set primary dates different to those envisaged by the DNC. This shows the limited power of national parties in America, even in presidential elections.

Box 1.2 Comments on the new rule changes for the Democratic primary calendar

'This is a significant effort to make the presidential primary nominating process more reflective of the diversity of this country, and to have issues that will determine the outcome of the November election part of the early process.'
(Rep. Debbie Dingell, (D) Michigan)

'We can proudly say that we sought to elevate the voices that have far too long been side-lined.'
(Rep. Nikema Williams, (D) Georgia state party chair)

The Republicans

Donald Trump may have been the former president, but he had also lost to Joe Biden once, been impeached by the House of Representatives twice, and was the subject of four criminal inquiries. If he thought he was going to have the Republican nomination race all to himself, Trump was about to be disappointed as between February and June 2023, nine other people declared their candidacies (see Table 1.3).

Donald Trump was the first to announce – straight after the 2022 midterm elections, in which the Republicans had not done as well as they had hoped. Indeed, many of Trump's endorsed candidates had been defeated. The Republicans had failed to win back control of the Senate and had won by only a very small majority in the House. So Trump's reputation had not exactly been enhanced. But it was inevitable he would seek a rematch with Biden, and the announcement duly came on 15 November 2022.

Table 1.3 Republican presidential candidates 2024 in order of entry

Candidate	Previous/current post	Entered race	Left race
Donald Trump	President	15/11/22	Nominated
Nikki Haley	Governor of South Carolina	14/2/23	6/3/24 (9)
Vivek Ramaswamy	Entrepreneur	21/2/23	15/1/24 (6)
Asa Hutchinson	Governor of Arkansas	26/4/23	16/1/24 (7)
Ron DeSantis	Governor of Florida	4/5/23	21/1/24 (8)
Tim Scott	US Senator, South Carolina	19/5/23	12/11/23 (2)
Mike Pence	Vice President	5/6/23	28/11/23 (3)
Chris Christie	Governor of New Jersey	6/6/23	10/1/24 (5)
Doug Burgum	Governor of North Dakota	7/6/23	4/12/23 (4)
Will Hurd	US Representative, Texas	22/6/23	9/10/23 (1)

We can divide the other nine candidates who joined the race during the first half of 2023 into two groups – the serious and the peripheral. The 'serious' were Nikki Haley and Ron DeSantis. The 'peripheral' were all the others. Indeed, five of them proved to be so peripheral that they pulled out before even a vote was cast in a primary or a caucus. Then, both Ramaswamy and

Hutchinson pulled out as soon as the results in Iowa were announced, and DeSantis was gone before New Hampshire voted eight days later. Thus, by the time New Hampshire's Republican voters went to the polls on 23 January, only Trump and Haley remained, showing once more how critical the 'invisible primary' period is in the whittling down of the field. These days, it's not the primaries which thin the field, but the pre-primary.

So how does that work? How is the field thinned out without a single vote being cast? The answer is through what one might call a political triangle of opinion polls, fundraising and media appearances – and those three feed off each other. High poll numbers lead to better fundraising which gives access to the media. Similarly, poor poll numbers lead to lower fundraising which leads to exclusion from the media. And this is most clearly on show in the intraparty TV debates staged between August 2023 and early January 2024.

This time round the Republicans staged five intra-party debates. In order to attend a debate, a candidate had to fulfil two criteria – relating to fundraising and poll numbers – as well as sign a 'loyalty pledge' to support the party's eventual presidential nominee. Table 1.4 shows the attendees at each of the five debates and it clearly shows that this is when the field of candidates is pruned – not in the primaries themselves.

Table 1.4 Attendees at the Republican intra-party TV debates

Date	Total	Attendees
23 August 2023	8	Burgum, Christie, DeSantis, Haley, Hutchinson, Pence, Ramaswamy, Scott
27 September	7	Burgum, Christie, DeSantis, Haley, Pence, Ramaswamy, Scott
8 November	5	Christie, DeSantis, Haley, Ramaswamy, Scott
6 December	4	Christie, DeSantis, Haley, Ramaswamy
10 January 2024	2	DeSantis, Haley

As for Donald Trump, he boycotted all five of these debates, often staging his own media event to clash with them. Some doubted the wisdom of this decision. After all, it left the field open for other candidates to attack him unchallenged, and it would deprive him of debate practice before facing

Biden in any presidential debates later in 2024. But Trump reckoned he didn't need to attend. His poll numbers were holding up very well without his attendance. He felt it made him look 'presidential'. But the big question was, 'What would happen when real voters started to have their say?'

CHAPTER 2

THE PRIMARIES

What you need to know

- Presidential primaries are state-based elections held between February and June of the presidential election year.
- They give ordinary voters a chance to say who they would like to be their party's candidate in the upcoming presidential election.
- Voters in the primaries also choose delegates to go to the national party conventions held in the summer, which is where the final decision about the candidate is made.
- A few sparsely-populated states hold caucuses rather than a primary.
- Caucuses are a series of meetings held across the state which perform the same functions as primaries.

In 2024, President Trump had a huge advantage over his Republican rivals. He was, after all, the former president who had used both his time in Washington and his time since leaving office to gain almost complete control of the levers of power within the Republican Party. His every whim was taken as the party's command. Indeed, it would be true to say that Trump was annoyed that *anyone* had dared challenge him for the party's presidential nomination, let alone that *nine* people had. But as we saw in Chapter 1, by the time the voting actually started, he had already seen off all but Nikki Haley and Ron DeSantis.

Iowa caucuses

Despite the changes that the Democrats had made in their primary calendar, the Republicans stuck with what they saw as the tried and tested schedule of letting Iowa and New Hampshire vote first. So, all Republican eyes were on Iowa for their state party caucuses on 15 January. Eight years earlier, Trump (24%) had struggled in Iowa – coming in second behind Senator Ted Cruz of Texas (27%) and beating Senator Marco Rubio of Florida (23%) by only one percentage point. But by 2024, Iowa was Trump Country and his win by over 30 percentage points (see Table 2.2) was a record for any contested Iowa Republican caucus. Winning with 51% of the vote in a seven-candidate race he won in 98 of Iowa's 99 counties. Trump's huge win denied the chance of generating early momentum to both Haley and DeSantis. Exit polling showed Trump winning almost every demographic group. The only clear exceptions were moderate and more liberal voters, as well as highly educated voters, who supported Haley. Another piece of good news for Trump was that in the eight days between the Iowa caucuses and the New Hampshire primary, DeSantis ended his bid for the nomination and endorsed Trump. Only Nikki Haley now stood between Trump and the Republican presidential nomination.

New Hampshire primary and beyond

There was, therefore, all to play for in New Hampshire on 23 January. Opinion polls showed the race closer than in Iowa but Trump was well ahead. But New Hampshire voters have a history of springing surprises in their presidential primaries. Would another be in store now? Almost! The results showed Trump beating Haley by 54% to 43%. Table 2.1 shows some of the voter groups in which Haley bettered Trump but, as column 1 shows, all of them are 'minority' groups. Nonetheless, this data did show up potential weaknesses for Trump in November.

Table 2.1 Groups in which Haley beat Trump in New Hampshire (Source: Exit poll)

Group (% of the electorate)	Trump (%)	Haley (%)
Urban (9%)	43	52
Not in full-time work (33%)	47	51
College graduate (48%)	42	56
First-time voter (16%)	30	65
Moderate/liberal (33%)	22	74
Late-deciders (18%)	35	61
Non-gun owners (45%)	43	53
Think Biden legitimately won in 2020 (46%)	22	76
Abortion the most important issue (12%)	26	66

Table 2.2 Republican primary results

Date	State	Trump %	Haley %
15 January	Iowa (C)	51	19
23 January	New Hampshire	54	43
24 February	South Carolina	59	39
27 February	Michigan	68	27
2 March	Idaho (C)	85	13
3 March	District of Columbia	33	**63**
4 March	North Dakota (C)	84	14
5 March	Alabama	83	13
	Alaska (C)	88	12
	Arkansas	77	18
	California	78	18
	Colorado	63	33
	Maine	73	25
	Massachusetts	60	37
	Minnesota	69	29
	North Carolina	74	23
	Oklahoma	82	16
	Tennessee	77	20
	Texas	78	17
	Utah (C)	56	43
	Vermont	46	**50**
	Virginia	63	35
6 March	*Nikki Haley suspends campaign*		
12 March	Georgia	84	13
	Hawaii (C)	97	-
	Mississippi	93	5
	Washington	76	19
19 March	Arizona	79	18
	Florida	81	14
	Illinois	81	14
	Kansas	75	16
	Ohio	79	14
23 March	Louisiana	90	7

2 April	Connecticut	**78**	14
	New York	**82**	13
	Rhode Island	**84**	11
	Wisconsin	**79**	13
23 April	Pennsylvania	**83**	17
7 May	Indiana	**78**	22
14 May	Maryland	**77**	23
	Nebraska	**80**	18
	West Virginia	**88**	9
21 May	Kentucky	**85**	6
4 June	Montana	**89**	-
	New Mexico	**82**	10

KEY: (C) = Caucuses; **Bold** = winner

But Nikki Haley had really bet the house on New Hampshire feeling this was her best – maybe her only – chance to at least slow the Trump bandwagon. She had enjoyed an on-off relationship with Donald Trump. Back in 2017, Trump had nominated her to be the US Ambassador to the United Nations, and Haley had resigned halfway through her second term as state governor to take up the post. But she resigned from the UN post the following year, continuing to call Trump 'a friend' but being mildly critical of some of Trump's excesses during the final months of his presidency.

However, Nikki Haley running in the 2024 presidential primary was breaking something of a glass ceiling in Republican presidential politics. After all, Haley was a woman, born to immigrant Sikh parents from India, hardly the most promising background for a Republican presidential candidate, even in the 21st century. The Republicans have never nominated a female presidential candidate. And since 1900, they have nominated 24 different vice-presidential candidates of which only one was a woman – Governor Sarah Palin of Alaska in 2008.

But even in the Republican primary in her home state of South Carolina where she had twice been elected governor, polls showed her with little chance of denting Trump's commanding lead. On the day, he beat her by 20 percentage points. After that, it was merely a question of how long she could last out. There were two victories to be enjoyed by Haley – in Washington DC (3 March) and Vermont (5 March) – but the day after that last victory she suspended her campaign. What was surprising was that even in the contests that came after her withdrawal, she still regularly attracted a vote share in double digits. A week later, Donald Trump secured enough delegates to be assured of his party's presidential nomination for the third time.

True, this nomination was harder fought than in 2020, but it was still relatively straightforward. So why was this the case? Let's consider three main reasons.

1. *The anti-Trump vote was divided*, just as it was back in 2016. Five of Trump's rivals – Haley, DeSantis, Christie, Hutchinson and Pence – were critical of the former president to varying degrees. Hence the anti-Trump support, which was always a minority amongst Republican supporters – and certainly amongst Republican primary voters – was made less effective.

2. *Trump had imposed his considerable authority and control on both the national party and state Republican parties.* Nowhere was this more clearly seen than just two days after Super Tuesday when there was a major personnel shake-up at the Republican National Committee (RNC). 'RNC installs new leadership as Trump tightens hold on party,' headlined the Politico website. The new co-chair of the RNC was to be Lara Trump, Donald Trump's daughter-in-law. The new chief operating officer was to be Chris LaCivita, Trump's senior campaign adviser.

3. During his years as president and in his post-White House years in Florida, *Trump had consolidated his hold over the Republican 'base'.* Indeed, one could say that Trump's Make America Great Again (MAGA) movement and the Republican Party were by now indistinguishable from one another. And because Trump controlled the party base, he controlled the party officials – both elected and appointed. Most anti-Trump Republicans had either walked away from politics, been defeated, marginalised or silenced.

The Democrats

Of course, there were Democratic primaries in 2024 as well, though they received very little media coverage. As we saw in Chapter 1, President Biden managed to avoid any significant intra-party opposition. By the time the primaries kicked off in February, Robert Kennedy was running as an independent candidate, not as a Democrat. Congressman Phillips pulled out the day after Super Tuesday and endorsed President Biden. In only two primaries did any candidate other than President Biden receive a share of the vote in double digits – Phillips winning 19% in New Hampshire and 13% in Ohio. But because New Hampshire Democrats had scheduled their primary in January – despite the DNC ruling it should not be held until early February – this was a meaningless vote as no convention delegates were awarded as a result of it. It was what we call a 'non-binding primary' or 'beauty contest'. And the vote in Ohio came after Phillips had withdrawn and endorsed Biden.

But there was one concern even at this stage for President Biden, and that was that in many primaries one could vote 'uncommitted' or 'none of the above'. And in nine primaries, 'uncommitted' or its equivalent polled over 10% – reaching 15% in Rhode Island, and 29% in Hawaii. As Figure 2.1 shows, Biden did not perform as well in the primaries as either Trump in 2020 or Obama in 2012 when they ran for re-election. True, Biden performed better than Ford, Carter and George H.W. Bush all of whom went on to lose in November. But his 87% support in the primaries was the lowest figure for an incumbent president seeking re-election for over 30 years. That was the first sign of a problem for Biden, that many Democratic primary voters remained unconvinced that the incumbent 81-year-old President was the candidate with the best chance of defeating Donald Trump in November. But at this stage, concerns about 'the age issue' were dismissed out of hand both by the White House and the Biden campaign. There were quiet mutterings about the fact that even Democrat-leaning voters were largely unenthused about another Biden candidacy. There was talk of 'the double-haters' – voters who 'hated', or at least were unenthusiastic about, both Biden and Trump. But it would take an event in late June to dramatically change the standing of President Biden amongst the leaders of his own party.

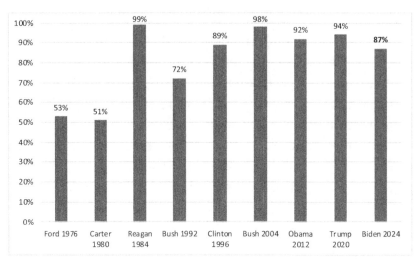

Figure 2.1 Incumbent presidents' share of the primary vote, 1976–2024

Caucuses

Finally, a word about caucuses. One wonders whether we're approaching the time when we can stop talking about them altogether. They now play such a minute part in the process. Caucuses – time-limited meetings held of an evening in schoolrooms or halls – were used in sparsely populated and geographically large states in which keeping hundreds, maybe thousands, of polling stations open all day for the handful of voters who might be in reach of them was regarded as impractical. The trouble was that caucuses attracted very low and highly unrepresentative turnout. For example, caucus voters tended to be drawn from the ideological extremes of the parties. And often there was no secret ballot. Voting was done by a show of hands. Results were difficult to tabulate and the process sometimes went awry. Hence the rise of primaries. In 1984, 23 states held Democratic primaries. By 2004, that had increased to 39. In 2024, it was 47, with only Hawaii, Idaho and Wyoming holding caucuses. On the Republican side, the number of states holding caucuses in 2024 was six – the three just mentioned, plus Iowa, North Dakota and Utah. The percentage of national convention delegates chosen in caucuses in 2024 was just 7% for the Republicans and a mere 1% for the Democrats. They have now been consigned to the very fringes of presidential politics.

Frontloading

One of the main reasons why the thinning of the candidates now occurs during the 'invisible primary' rather than during the primaries themselves is because of frontloading. In a period of just 15 days – between 5 and 19 March – 58% of the delegates to the Democratic Convention and 61%

of the delegates to the Republican Convention were chosen. During that period, there were 22 Democratic and 24 Republican primaries. As Table 2.3 shows, by the end of the third week in March, the vast majority of national convention delegates for both parties had already been chosen, yet the primaries had another two-and-a-half months to run. So, although in theory the primaries are stretched out over four months, in practice everything is decided in a fortnight towards the start of the process. That's what we call frontloading.

This has a number of important consequences.

1. It favours well-known, well-financed candidates.
2. It significantly reduces the ability of the primaries to test the presidential qualities of would-be candidates.
3. It favours the large-population states and renders the small states almost powerless.
4. It reduces the opportunity of voters in later-voting states to have 'second thoughts' as they mull over the decisions made in the earlier contests.
5. It means the general election campaign begins earlier as the parties' candidates are now usually finalised by March or April.

Table 2.3 Cumulative percentage of national convention delegates chosen, by week, to 23 March

Week ending	Cumulative percentage of delegates chosen	
	Democratic Party	Republican Party
20 January	0	2
27 January	0	3
3 February	0	3
10 February	2	3
17 February	2	4
24 February	2	4
2 March	5	8
9 March	41	47
16 March	48	54
23 March	53	69

But it's impossible to see any meaningful change coming in future election cycles. Some have proposed monthly regional primaries – such as the South in March; the Northeast in April; the Midwest in May; the West in June – to make the primaries a more thoughtful and deliberative process. But in 2024, the Democratic National Committee struggled even to rearrange the dates of the primaries in New Hampshire and Georgia making any wholesale changes seem highly unlikely. Major reform of the presidential nomination process may be much needed, but it's highly unlikely to occur. The chances are we shall continue to see only the four-yearly tinkering with the process whilst the underlying problems remain.

CHAPTER 3

THE BIDEN–TRUMP DEBATE

> **What you need to know**
> - Televised presidential debates began in the election of 1960 between John F. Kennedy (D) and Richard Nixon (R).
> - There were no TV debates in 1964, 1968 or 1972.
> - In the elections between 1976 and 2020, there were at least two presidential debates. In those elections, there was also one vice-presidential debate except in 1980.
> - From 1976 to 1984, the debates were sponsored by the League of Women voters. From 1988 to 2020, they were organised by the Commission on Presidential Debates.

It was mid-May of 2024. The primaries were pretty much done and dusted. Joe Biden and Donald Trump were the presumptive presidential nominees of their respective parties. But with over three months still to the traditional start of the general election campaign at the start of September and the polls showing the race between the two leading candidates both close and static, the Biden campaign decided to try and shake things up a bit. Their idea of how to 'shake things up a bit' was announced on 15 May when President Biden announced that he would not take part in the traditional televised presidential debates organised by the Commission on Presidential Debates (CPD) in the autumn, but instead challenged Trump to two debates – one in June, and another in September. Little did Biden realise the unintended consequences of this seemingly ingenious plan, for hidden within it was an existential threat to his very candidacy.

Setting the scene

By 2024, televised presidential debates had got themselves something of a bad name. Many considered them over-hyped and less than useful. They rarely had a significant effect on the final outcome of the election, although there had been exceptions. They were about style more than substance. The audiences had become raucous and a distraction from any serious debate over policy. The CPD who had organised them for nearly 40 years came in for much criticism from the candidates of both parties, as well as from the wider electorate. The 2020 debates between Biden and Trump were regarded as the worst of them all. As Donald Trump, the presumptive Republican nominee, had boycotted all the Republican debates (see Chapter 1) and President Biden, the presumptive Democratic nominee, was not a great fan of debates at all, there was much early speculation that 2024 might be the death knell of them.

A new format

So there was some surprise when the Biden and Trump campaigns announced the dates of two debates, and even more surprise when the details of them were revealed. The two campaigns had agreed to two debates – nothing too unusual there. But then came the four surprises.

1. ***The debates would not be organised by the CPD, but by TV networks*** – the first by CNN and the second by ABC.

2. ***The first debate would be before the national party conventions.*** Never before had a TV debate been held before mid-September. But this time, the first debate was to be on 27 June, with the second on 10 September. Clearly, neither campaign wanted a late debate with the chance that a poor performance by their candidate could lose them the election. Also, with so much early voting these days, debates in late October make no sense as by that time a significant proportion of the electorate will already have voted.

3. ***There would be no studio audience*** – something that observers were surprised that the Trump campaign had agreed to as Donald Trump was known to be energised by an audience – the more raucous the better.

4. After the experience of Trump's frequent interruptions of and talking over Biden in 2020, this time ***microphones would be muted*** except when it was that candidate's turn to be speaking.

Then there was the question of which candidates would be invited. This was important in an election in which three independent or third-party candidates were featuring in opinion polls, even if their support was in the single digits. The rules set by CNN for the first debate were two-fold. To be invited a candidate had to:

- appear on the ballots of enough states to earn the requisite 270 Electoral College votes needed to win the presidency; and
- win at least 15% support in four national opinion polls.

Whether by coincidence or design, none of the third-party candidates met these hurdles, so it would be a debate between only Biden and Trump.

Debate night

On Thursday 27 June at 9pm on the east coast – 6pm on the west coast – around 51 million Americans tuned in to watch the Biden–Trump debate, well below the estimated figure of 73 million who watched the first Trump–Biden debate in September 2020. Indeed, it was the lowest viewership for the opening debate of a presidential election cycle since the 46.6 million who tuned it to watch the first debate between George W. Bush and Al Gore in 2000 (see Figure 3.1).

Figure 3.1 Viewership (millions) for first presidential debates, 1960–2024

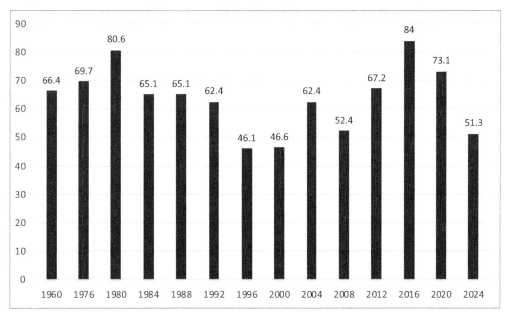

The format seemed a great improvement from what presidential debates had degenerated into by 2020. Getting rid of the studio audience was in most people's view a big improvement. The audiences had turned the debates into 'entertainment' rather than serious political debate. Muting the other candidate's microphone whilst one candidate was speaking was also a huge improvement and stopped candidates from talking over, interrupting or shouting at their opponent as Trump had done incessantly to both Hillary Clinton in 2016 and Joe Biden in 2020.

Biden's stumbling performance

But when the 90 minutes ended, that was not what commentators – or the viewers at home – were talking about. Post-debate comment and evaluation was focused on the stumbling performance of President Biden. Having watched pretty much every presidential debate since the Ford–Carter debate in 1976, I had never seen a performance as poor as this. For sure, some candidates had made gaffes which damaged their campaigns, but never before had one of the candidates given such a halting, stumbling and at times incoherent performance as President Biden did on that evening.

Box 3.1 Debate analysis

'The problem for Biden from this debate tonight is the collective freak-out from Democrats is at the highest level you can imagine. This is the problem for Biden. It's not where the 'double-haters' or the undecided voters go. It's that the Democratic base itself, the donors, the folks who are down-ballot [Senators, House members, Governors, etc. also running for re-election], those are the ones who are depressed and anxious, and that is not helpful to Biden this close to the election.'

Amy Walter of 'The Cook Political Report with Amy Walter,' on the PBS NewsHour

Two moments – both quite early on in the debate – stood out. The first came when moderator Jake Tapper asked Joe Biden to respond to Donald Trump's answer about the national debt. Referring to Trump's four years as president, Biden began:

He had the largest national debt of any president four-year period, number one. Number two, he got $2 trillion tax cut, benefitted the very wealthy. What I'm going to do is fix the taxes. For example, we have a thousand trillionaires in America – I mean, billionaires in America. And what's happening? They're in a situation where they, in fact, pay 8.2% in taxes. If they just paid 24% or 25%, either one of those numbers, they'd raise $500 million – billion dollars, I should say, in a ten-year period.

Not the clearest or most coherent answer, but just about comprehensible. But then Biden seemed to completely lose his train of thought. He continued:

We'd be able to right – wipe out his debt. We'd be able to make sure that all those things we need to do, childcare, elder care, making sure we continue to strengthen our healthcare system, making sure we're able to make every single solitary person eligible for what I've been able to do with the Covid – excuse me, with dealing with everything we have to do with ... Look if ... We finally beat Medicare.

This was nothing short of alarming. Former President Trump pounced.

'Well, he's right, he did beat Medicare. He beat it to death. And he's destroying Medicare.'

A few minutes later, Jake Tapper introduced a new segment of the debate on the issue of immigration and border security. He asked President Biden why, given the current record numbers of migrants crossing the border from Mexico into the United States during his presidency, voters should trust him to solve the crisis. The President attempted an answer before saying:

What I've done – since I've changed the law, what's happened? I've changed it in a way that now you're in a situation where there are 40% fewer people coming across the border illegally. It's better than when he left office. And I'm going to continue to move until we get the total ban on the – the total initiative relative to what we're going to do with more Border Patrol and more asylum officers.

The last few words were uttered by the President in a somewhat bemused way. His words were halting, disjointed. Cutaway shots showed President Trump twice turning towards President Biden with a puzzled look on his face, as if Trump was thinking, 'What is going on? What's happening? What's he trying to say?' Jake Tapper invited President Trump to respond: 'I really don't know what he said at the end of that sentence. I don't think he knows what he said either.' In the first debate with Joe Biden back in 2020, Trump had been rude, shouty and full of bluster. It even put off a number of Republican voters.

Now, here was Trump appearing to be more presidential than the President! Trump couldn't believe his luck.

Election-watchers tend to look for what we call the 'bounce' that a candidate receives from such an event as this – especially the *first* debate. By a 'bounce' we mean the increase in the percent of those supporting their candidacy in the first opinion poll held after the debate compared with the last poll before the debate. The rule of thumb is that challengers tend to gain more of a 'bounce' than incumbents because they don't have a record to defend. But with the candidates in 2024 being an incumbent president and a former president, a 'bounce' for either candidate seemed unlikely. But as Table 3.1 shows, it was former President Trump who came out better in the 'bounce' stakes gaining a positive bounce of 2.2 percentage points.

Table 3:1 Pre- and post-first televised debate polls compared

	Biden	Trump	State of the race
27 June poll	40.9%	41.1%	Trump + 0.2
4 July poll	39.7%	42.1%	Trump + 2.4
Change	-1.2	+1.0	Trump + 2.2

[Source: projects.fivethirtyeight.com/polls/]

Even more significantly, Biden's awful performance in the debate sent shock waves through the higher echelons of the Democratic Party. It appeared to many that the President no longer had the mental sharpness and verbal coherence to prosecute a case against Donald Trump. And as another Trump presidency was being portrayed by the Democrats – even by Biden himself – as tantamount to the 'end of democracy' in America, something had to give.

Table 3.2 Question asked of Democrats: 'Does President Biden have the mental capacity to be an effective president?'

	22-26 February	11-15 July
Extremely/very confident	40%	27%
Somewhat confident	27%	25%
Not very/not at all confident	32%	48%

[Source: apnorc.org/projects, 17 July 2024]

But doubts were not only to be found amongst the Democratic Party leadership. It was the same amongst would-be Democratic voters. An Associated Press-NORC Poll conducted between 11–15 July showed some alarming results. When asked, 'Should Joe Biden withdraw from the race and allow his party to select a different candidate?' 65% of Democrats said 'yes'. Amongst Democrat voters aged 18–44, the figure rose to 75%! When pollsters asked would-be Democrat voters, 'Does President Biden have the mental capacity to be an effective president?' whereas in February 40% had said they were extremely or very confident that he did, the figure now in July was only 27% (see Table 3.2). And whereas in February, just under one-third of Democrats said they were not very or not at all confident of Biden's mental capacity to be an effective president, now in July it was just under a half.

The irony was that it had been President Biden who had wanted the debate, who had been the driving force behind getting it arranged, and who wanted it this early in the election cycle. He had wanted it so that he could draw a strong and positive contrast with Donald Trump. But the whole thing had badly backfired. It was now Republicans who were elated and Democrats who were utterly depressed. There followed 25 days of utter turmoil within the Democratic Party which would result in the first exit of a sitting president from his re-election campaign since President Johnson exited in March 1968.

CHAPTER 4

BIDEN'S EXIT

What you need to know

- Biden's departure at such a late stage of the presidential campaign was unprecedented in modern US politics.
- There had been some long-term concerns about his age and physical/cognitive abilities and running for and winning the 2024 election.
- The disastrous election debate with Donald Trump in June was pivotal to the growing pressure on Biden to pull out of the race.
- Biden stayed in the race for nearly four weeks after the televised debate.
- Among the key groups pressuring him to step down were congressional Democrats but also significant donors.
- Arguably the single biggest argument used to persuade Biden to step down was the growing likelihood of a Trump victory if he stayed on the ticket, and the electoral damage to Democrats seeking election or re-election to Congress.
- Biden immediately endorsed his vice president, Kamala Harris, as his preferred choice as the Democrat nominee.

Context and precedence

'I shall not seek, and I will not accept, the nomination of my party for another term as your President.' These were the words of a Democrat president withdrawing from the presidential race following increasing divisions and disquiet about their candidacy. But the year was 1968 and the president was Lyndon B. Johnson (LBJ), and the announcement was made in March, over four months away from the party convention in August that would nominate his successor. Similarly, back pedal to 1952 and Harry Truman, another Democrat president withdrew from running for a second (full) term. He too announced his decision to quit in March, months before the convention. Truman had also apparently made his decision to quit three years earlier writing a memorandum to himself early in 1950: 'Eight years as President is enough.'

It is not without precedent then for serving presidents to pull out of re-election races having already committed themselves to running for that second term. Why was Biden's exit different to those of both LBJ and Truman? Also, what was the one key similarity?

- Biden's withdrawal came very late in the day, barely a month away from the convention itself which would have formally crowned him as the Democrat nominee.

- Both LBJ and Truman pulled out following early primary setbacks. Both men had fared poorly in the New Hampshire primary. Biden by contrast, as we have seen, largely cruised through the Democrat primaries, though with the caveat that his support among Democrat primary voters was lower than for many of his recent predecessors (see Chapter 2). That said, Phillips, Williamson and Kennedy lacked a broad popular following among the Democrat grassroots, unlike Eugene McCarthy who had attracted a strong following among younger Democrats due to his anti-war stance on Vietnam back in 1968. Voting 'uncommitted' in the 2024 Democrat primaries sent a message, but it hardly echoed with senior Democrats who steadfastly backed Biden throughout the primary season.

- The opposition within the Democrat Party that led to Truman and LBJ ending their re-election bids was primarily ideological in nature. This was truest for LBJ whose escalation of US military involvement in Vietnam caused huge divisions among Democrats. For Biden, the opposition was primarily based on his fitness – both physical and mental – to win the election. It was more personal than policy. While most Democrats held a deep affection for Biden for his long service in Congress, as VP and defeating Trump in 2020, increasingly it was his abilities as an effective campaigner that piled on the pressure. Many of those arguing for him to step down, or more diplomatically, to reconsider his nomination, did so with a clear tinge of regret. West Virginia senator Joe Manchin surely drew an accurate comparison when he said Democrats were acting out of affection for Biden, 'much as a family persuading an aging grandparent to surrender the car keys.' An electoral car crash needed to be avoided.

This brings us to the one similarity linking all three Democrat withdrawals: the likelihood of impending defeat in November. Both Truman and LBJ were unpopular candidates nationally, who were deemed increasingly unlikely to win against strong Republican opponents, Eisenhower and Nixon respectively. No presidential candidate can ignore unfavourable polls, and polls pile on the political pressure. In the months before his withdrawal, Biden enjoyed an average approval rating of under 40%. It was 38.5% according to the final poll before his decision to pull out of the race. He also lagged behind Trump in key battleground states including Nevada, Arizona and Pennsylvania.

Box 4.1 Key events in Biden's exit during 2024

7 March. Biden delivered the State of the Union address. It was well received by Democrats and reassured some doubters in their ranks. Biden even addressed the age issue – to his own advantage: 'When you get to be my age, certain things become clearer than ever ... My lifetime has taught me to embrace freedom and democracy future based on core values that have defined America: honesty, decency, dignity, equality.'

27 June. Biden delivered a somewhat incoherent performance in his first televised debate with Trump (see Chapter 3).

28 June. Biden spoke at a Democrat rally in North Carolina reaffirming his decision to stay in the race. 'I intend to win this election. When you get knocked down, you get back up,' Biden said, alluding to his debate performance a day earlier. He went on to justify his decision to stay in the race, focusing on how he believed Trump represented a threat to US democracy saying, 'I know I'm not a young man, to state the obvious. I would not be running again if I didn't believe with all my heart and soul that I could do this job. The stakes are too high.'

2 July. Lloyd Doggett, a Democrat House member from Texas, became the first congressional Democrat to urge publicly for Biden to quit the race. He would be followed by at least 30 others over the following days.

5 July. In a 22-minute interview on CNN, Biden again defended his record and ability to run for a second term. He emphatically denied he was thinking of leaving the race. In his own words, 'If the Lord Almighty came down and said, "Joe, get out of the race," I'd get out of the race. The Lord Almighty's not coming down.' Pressed whether his allies within the party might ask him to stand aside, 'It's not going to happen,' he said.

10 July. George Clooney, actor, Hollywood A-lister and a major Democrat donor, called on Biden to leave the race. Recalling a fundraiser he hosted with the President in Los Angeles he said: 'It's devastating to say it, but the Joe Biden I was with three weeks ago at the fundraiser was not the Joe Biden of 2010. He wasn't even the Joe Biden of 2020. He was the same man we all witnessed at the debate.'

11 July. At a NATO summit, he mistakenly introduced Ukrainian president Volodymyr Zelensky as 'President Putin'.

13 July. Democratic Senate leader Charles Schumer and Biden met for 35 minutes at the President's vacation home in Delaware. Schumer conveyed his colleagues' deep concerns and how some might go public with their views. Biden, accounts suggest, was taken aback and asked Schumer to give him a week.

17 July. Biden tested positive for Covid and was forced to take several days off the campaign trail.

21 July. Biden announced his withdrawal from the contest and endorsed Harris.

24 July. Biden explained his reasons for leaving the race in a nationwide broadcast, with references to uniting his party, saving US democracy and 'passing the torch to a new generation'.

Analysis: Why did Biden withdraw?

There was no single factor to explain Biden's exit from the 2024 presidential race but ultimately it was down to the polls and predictions. When it came down to it, too many senior Democrat figures worried that Biden, despite his protestations, was simply 'not up to it'. The televised debate will probably, with hindsight, be seen as the decisive moment when the worst fears of his fellow Democrats were confirmed. They were not convinced that one poor performance on national television was an outlier. Existing concerns had been charitably put to one side prior to the debate, perhaps too charitably. Events in the days that followed did nothing to dispel such fears. Catching Covid, while hardly his fault, was probably the last straw. Anything else, including increasingly desperate ploys to keep donors and congressional Democrats loyal, smacked of desperation.

If those in senior roles could not unsee what they had seen in the debate, the actual timing of Biden's departure was probably forced by Democrat senators. Biden evoked considerable loyalty among Democrat senators, he had after all been one of their number for over three decades. The Senate is also a place where seniority and longstanding loyalties still count for a lot. Yet when even Rhode Island senator Jack Reed, not known as a troublemaker or political rival of Biden, spoke first at a private meeting on 11 July, the die was probably cast. He reportedly said that if Biden wanted to stay in the race, he should submit to examination by two independent neurologists who were willing to report their findings at a news conference. Of the dozen or so Democrats who spoke at that meeting, only three spoke up for Biden remaining as candidate. Ultimately, it was the likelihood of public statements questioning his fitness to remain, that convinced Biden to throw in the towel. A trickle of publicly disloyal statements up till then, could become a flood.

Alongside all this, former House Speaker Nancy Pelosi, another powerful figure in the top circles of the Democrat Party with an extensive political network, had also expressed her reservations and applied pressure behind the scenes. It was reported that she had urged fellow Democrats to 'speak their conscience'. While she never went public calling for his withdrawal, neither was she one of his last firm supporters.

So ultimately, there was no one figure or factor in Biden's exit from the race. It was though the removal of support from the political elites, that sealed his fate. Biden remained stubborn, unable perhaps to grasp that his closest allies really were ready to pull the rug. They talked of doing this to protect his own legacy and to enable him to go with some dignity. The reality was perhaps more about political self-preservation. For some it was personal; for all it was about the interests of the wider party.

CHAPTER 5

SELECTING A RUNNING MATE

What you need to know

- Each presidential candidate chooses their own vice-presidential candidate, otherwise known as their 'running mate'.
- They run for election together as 'a joint ticket'.
- Running mates are often chosen to 'balance the ticket' – balance in such areas as geographic region, age, ideology, political experience, religion or gender.
- The running mates are confirmed by the party conventions.
- Typically, running mates have little effect in determining the outcome of the election.

Introduction

In the introduction to her 2020 book *Picking the Vice President*, Elaine Kamarck recalls a scene from the popular HBO series *VEEP* where the (fictional) vice president, Selina Meyer, becomes irritated that the President has not called her. Frustrated, she asks a former Senate colleague, 'What have I been missing here?' to which the instant if disconcerting reply is 'Power!'

Traditionally, the role of understudy to the occupant of the White House has been somewhat peripheral. The Constitution is silent on their role beyond their vital function of being ready to step, at a moment's notice, into the presidential shoes should disaster or a general anaesthetic befall. The latter is a direct reference to the fact that when the president has to undergo an emergency medical procedure requiring temporary loss of consciousness, the VP finds themselves thrust temporarily into the lead role. Some recent presidents – Clinton with Gore, and George W. Bush with Cheney – sought out running mates as potential active partners in government rather than merely 'balancing the ticket' and enhancing their chances of victory. For others, including in 2024, their selection owed more to how they enhance electability and be that vital 'second stage of the rocket' to lift the top of the ticket into presidential orbit. That may seem normal enough, but in reality, certain aspects of the VP selection process in 2024 were unusual.

2024 was different

There is nothing that unusual in both running mates being new to the role. The same was true in 2016 when both Mike Pence and Tim Kaine were chosen by Donald Trump and Hilary Clinton respectively. But in 2024 two things stand out:

1. Trump ditched his former 2016 and 2020 running mate (and VP, 2017–21), Mike Pence. This perhaps was hardly surprising as both men had fallen out over Pence's, entirely correct, decision to formally certify the results of the Electoral College just before the Capitol riot. In his memoirs from 2022, Pence noted Trump said that he (Pence) 'didn't have the courage to do what should have been done to protect our Country and our Constitution'. For Pence this was too much. He rightly saw his certification role as purely ceremonial. Unfortunately, his former boss and his supporters did not. Many of those storming the Capitol saw Pence as part of the plot to deny Trump victory. There were even placards with 'Hang Pence' written on them. It is not unknown for presidents or former presidents to switch running mates in their re-election bid – FDR dropped Henry Wallace in favour of Harry Truman in 1944 for example. But the circumstances of Pence's removal were pretty unique.

2. For Harris, the issue was one of urgency. While it is again not unusual for vice presidents to assume the role of president whether due to death (Johnson for Kennedy) or scandal (Ford for Nixon) and thus then scrabble around for a new deputy, it is unique in modern US history for this to occur between the primaries and the general election. Harris found herself at short notice needing not only to reinvent herself as a presidential nominee, but also to find a replacement for her own role.

In each case though, despite the unusual circumstances, both eventual nominees fitted the usual criteria in many respects. To adopt the language of A-level exam board comparative theories, they were 'rational choices'.

Why did Trump pick Vance?

The first thing to recall is that for many years Trump presented *The Apprentice*, where a long list of young hopefuls is whittled down by a series of challenges until only one is left. One suspects that Trump therefore rather enjoyed the selection process even if it did not quite follow the approach of its televised counterpart. Certainly, Trump and his key advisers started with a sizeable list of potential names, nearly two dozen by some accounts. Much time was spent vetting the names on the list. One staffer recalled how Trump and his top aides constantly sought out opinions on who the pick should be. 'If you met with him, he was going to ask you.'

Eventually, the list was narrowed down to three: Florida senator Marco Rubio; Governor Doug Burgum of North Dakota; and Ohio senator JD Vance. Before analysing why Vance was picked it is worth briefly noting the weaknesses of the other two contenders. With Rubio interestingly, a key sticking point was constitutional. The Twelfth Amendment clearly states that the president and vice president must reside in different states. Unfortunately, in this case, both Trump and Rubio resided in Florida. While some change of electoral registration might have been possible, it would doubtless have given rise to legal wranglings and potential court cases. For Burgum, the crunch issue was probably more political. Back in 2023 on the back of the Supreme Court's *Dobbs v Jackson* decision, Burgum signed a bill effectively banning abortions in his state, a measure harsher than those enacted in many red states including Florida. Trump called it a 'terrible mistake'. In an election where the Democrats would be keen to highlight abortion rights, Trump did not want to confront or defend the most radical actions undertaken by some of his fellow Republicans in their home states, especially that close to the presidential ticket.

So, what star qualities did Vance, the 40-year-old junior senator from Ohio, have that eluded his rivals?

1. **Youth**. At the time of his selection, Trump was still facing Biden. Hence the average age of the Trump/Vance ticket would be considerably lower than that of Biden/Harris.
2. **Appealing backstory**. Vance had already achieved some fame through his book *Hillbilly Elegy* charting his life from a troubled

upbringing in the Appalachians to military service in Iraq and thence to Yale Law School, culminating in becoming a venture capitalist and embarking on a career in Republican politics. This was a classic 'rags to riches' story emphasising the importance of hard work, faith and family, with criticisms of his peers who remained dependent on welfare benefits and who lacked any real work ethic.

3. **The zeal of a convert**. Vance had not always embraced Trump. Back in 2016, he had privately written on Facebook to a former law school roommate: 'I go back and forth between thinking Trump is a cynical a**hole ... or that he's America's Hitler.' From a never-Trumper to an always-Trumper makes for a classic conversion story.

4. **Media performance**. Apparently, what helped swing it for Trump and thus for Vance, was his performance on Fox News following Trump's visit to Ohio after a toxic train derailment.

5. **Geography**. Ohio is in that Midwest/Rust Belt area of the US, and although now largely trending Republican in presidential elections, Ohio is close to several key battleground states including Wisconsin, Michigan and Pennsylvania. Aides also calculated, correctly as it turned out, that were Biden to falter and be replaced by Harris, she too would pick a mid-Westerner for precisely the same electoral reasons.

6. **Loyalty**. Perhaps the trait most valued by Trump. Vance regardless of earlier misgivings, now shared pretty much the same values as his new boss. This applied most notably on trade, immigration and foreign policy. Vance was also particularly critical of continued US support for Ukraine. The loyal understudy is required to learn and repeat the script of the lead actor and not to write their own.

7. **Prominent supporters**. Donald Trump's sons, Eric and Donald Junior, were enthusiastic backers of Vance. In the court of Trump, such endorsements carried a lot of weight.

Why did Harris pick Walz?

If Trump had a degree of leisure during which to make his VP pick, no such luxury was available to Harris. The timeframe between Harris stepping up and the party convention in August when the ticket would be formally presented to delegates, was just 16 days.

The first thing Harris did was to tap former Attorney General Eric Holder, a veteran of the Obama administration, and Dana Remus, a former White House counsel for Biden, to lead the effort. Holder and a team of researchers ultimately vetted nine choices, less than ideal perhaps but sufficient. Among those considered were several serving governors beyond Walz, who it should be noted was not considered a frontrunner early on. They mostly came either from crucial swing states or held office in Midwest red states most notably Shapiro from Pennsylvania, Cooper from North Carolina, and Beshear from Kentucky. New(ish) Arizona senator and former astronaut, Mark Kelly, also made the short list. After Cooper privately dropped out, Kelly, Walz and Shapiro made the final cut and had a 90-minute interview with Harris.

Shapiro, a very good campaigner, was undermined somewhat by a less than glowing comment from his fellow Pennsylvania Democrat, Senator John Fetterman. Via an intermediary, he portrayed Shapiro as a political opportunist with his own ambitions. Also, Shapiro is Jewish, as incidentally is Harris' husband, Doug Emhoff. Usually this would not be an issue, but in the sensitive context of the Israel–Gaza war, it did play a part perhaps in reducing his chances. His own stance on the war was not fundamentally different from that of the other contenders – or from Harris herself – and he had also been harshly critical of Israeli Prime Minister Benjamin Netanyahu. But Shapiro was arguably perceived as more tied into a broadly pro-Israel position.

Table 5.1 Balancing the ticket – how each vice-presidential candidate 'balanced' and complemented their respective presidential nominee

Category	Vance (Trump)	Walz (Harris)
Gender	✗	✔
Age	✔	✗
Religion*	✔	✗
Ethnicity	✗	✔
Potential appeal in swing states	✔	✔
Geography/home state	✔	✔
Political experience**	✔	✔

*While Trump identifies as a Presbyterian (a Protestant Christian church), Vance is Roman Catholic. Harris meanwhile is a Baptist, while Walz is a Lutheran – both Protestant churches.

**Vance is a senator whilst Trump has never been a member of Congress. Walz has been both a member of the House of Representatives and latterly a governor. Harris meanwhile served as a senator before becoming vice president.

This in turn raised questions about whether he would draw the kinds of protests that Biden had faced from his left wing for continuing to send military weapons to Israel in its war against Hamas in Gaza. Kelly, meanwhile, was weakened by his stance on trade unions/organised labour, expressing reservations about pending labour legislation in Washington. This led some union leaders, such as the president of the United Auto Workers, who had publicly endorsed Harris, to have reservations about Kelly. Organised labour remains a big player in the Democrat world.

So much for the alleged weaknesses of his fellow contenders. What were the positives in favour of Walz's VP candidacy, a candidate who began very much on the longlist of potential running mates?

1. **Geography**. As with Vance, Walz hailed from the Midwest and those crucial battleground states. Although governor of strongly blue Minnesota, it too abuts key bellwether states.

2. **Influential supporters**. As with Vance, it helped Walz's cause that he had some powerful backers amongst the Democratic elites. Perhaps chief among these was Harris' fellow California Democrat, former House speaker Nancy Pelosi who worked below the radar to express support for Walz.

3. **Lived experience**. There is no doubt that Walz's background as a teacher, school sport's coach and National Guardsman helped. Add in a 'folksy' demeanour and what one BBC article called his 'balding, rotund, slightly dishevelled appearance'. He also spoke openly about the fertility challenges he and his wife had when conceiving their first child, which involved intrauterine insemination (IUI) treatment. With Democrats keen to get reproductive rights more widely near the top of the political agenda, that too could be seen as an advantage.

4. **The sound bite that resonated**. Just as with Vance, media performances matter when the presidential nominee makes their final pick. While

Biden's disastrous debate with Trump proved pivotal in his withdrawal from the race, Walz's one-liner during an appearance on MSNBC's *Morning Joe* went viral and struck a key chord with Harris and her team. He dubbed Trump and Vance as 'just weird'. The term became a buzz word in Democrat circles and helped propel him into that (largely) coveted No.2 slot. As one close aide put it: 'I think Walz just emerged as that person who she grew to trust and admire.'

So ultimately, Harris played it safe, selecting a running mate who would complement her strengths without causing friction within her party's ranks. As with Trump's pick, loyalty, shoring up party unity, a strong media performance and broader 'good vibes' were key in explaining her choice. The obvious frontrunners do not always make it through to the winner's enclosure.

CHAPTER 6
THE PARTY CONVENTIONS

What you need to know

- Party conventions are a key fixture in an election year, and in 2024 were unusually important for both parties.
- The Republican Convention took place two days after the assassination attempt on Donald Trump at a rally in Pennsylvania.
- The Democratic Convention had just witnessed the nomination of Kamala Harris as presidential candidate after President Biden withdrew from the race having won the primaries with ease.
- Conventions are mainly about showcasing the presidential ticket to the public and media, rather than deciding policy or choosing candidates. They are, in effect, stage-managed political rallies which offer the candidates the opportunity to define themselves and their policy vision and values.
- The party platform for each party is formally endorsed.
- The Republican Party enjoyed a post-convention 'bounce' in their poll ratings in 2024. The Democrats did not, although their 'bounce' occurred following Harris's entering the race.

The traditional function of conventions

The satirical magazine, *Private Eye*, recently summed up the modern US party convention very neatly. It stated that the point of such jamborees was 'for delegates to tour the country and meet people from Wyoming for the first time; for merchandise vendors to offload their dead stock of Biden or Mike Pence T-shirts; for the political parties, though, these are four-night infomercials, selling their prime slogans and personalities to a primetime television audience'.

Formally though, the prime function of party conventions in the US is officially nominating the presidential candidate and presenting their vice-presidential pick to a wider audience. To borrow the language of romance from social media, it is the official announcement that the partners on the election ticket are 'in a relationship'. Unsurprisingly therefore, the final part of the convention is a gathering of the candidates and their families on the platform to receive rapturous applause as the balloons drop from the convention hall roof. In reality, the 'political dating' had been going on a while before. Recent elections have seen the presidential nomination wrapped up well in advance, usually by the mid-point in the state primary calendar as we saw in Chapter 2.

The selection of the vice-presidential candidate is now announced ahead of the convention itself. There is no great 'reveal' on the convention floor. Donald Trump announced his pick of Ohio senator JD Vance on his social media platform, Truth Social, on the first day of the Republican convention but before it officially began. Tim Walz was announced as Kamala Harris's VP choice a full fortnight or so before the Democratic convention. Table 6.1 outlines some of the general roles played, and not played, by party conventions.

Table 6.1 The main roles/non-roles of party conventions in modern America

Role	True/ False	Explanation
Choose the party's presidential ticket for the November election	False	The nomination should have already been decided in advance via the primaries/ caucuses. If not, it becomes a 'brokered' or 'contested' convention. No recent convention has fallen into this category, despite coming close on occasions.
Securing publicity and media attention for the party ticket	True	Conventions are intended to showcase candidates and their vision for America. Sound bites and slogans are anticipated and thoroughly analysed by friends and foes alike.
Presenting a united image for the party	True	This is especially true after a gruelling and divisive primary season. Trump's main rival in 2024, Nikki Haley, spoke in his support at the Republican convention.

Deciding on policy	False	Party platforms will have been decided upon in advance. Indeed, much will already have been in evidence during primary debates and rallies. Divisions within the party make for bad publicity and are definitely not welcome at these events. The conventions do formally endorse the party's platform though.
Energise and motivate the party base	True	A successful convention leaves attendees fired up to support their party's candidates when they return home.
Help win the November election	True	For all the reasons listed above, plus geography. Convention locations are carefully chosen for electoral advantage (see opposite).

To this list we might add, the opportunity for delegates and the wider public to be treated to various performances and publicity stunts by individuals from the celebrity and entertainment worlds. There is also the opportunity to hear from those outside the political world – ordinary Americans who can 'tell their story' that reinforces the candidate's core messages and values. As with music festivals, another perennial summer fixture, a wide variety of performers are on offer, the vibe is positive throughout, the headline act plays the final night, and most folk go home with a lot of merch!

Convention location

Location is also traditionally a key consideration of conventions. Parties give a lot of thought to the city where the convention takes place. A recent rule of thumb, albeit broken by the Democrats in 2024, is to host it in a competitive state and maybe gain some local momentum. The table below summarises the recent locations of party conventions, whether they were 'in play' that election, and the final result.

Table 6.2 The location of Democratic and Republican conventions since 2000

Year	Party	Location	Competitive state that year?	State won by hosting party?
2024	Republican	Milwaukee, Wisconsin	Yes	Yes
	Democratic	Chicago, Illinois	No	Yes
2020*	Republican	Charlotte, North Carolina	Yes	Yes
	Democratic	Milwaukee, Wisconsin	Yes	Yes
2016	Republican	Cleveland, Ohio	Yes	Yes
	Democratic	Philadelphia, Pennsylvania	Yes	No
2012	Republican	Tampa, Florida	Yes	No
	Democratic	Charlotte, North Carolina	Yes	No
2008	Republican	St Paul, Minnesota	No	No
	Democratic	Denver, Colorado	Yes	Yes
2004	Republican	New York	No	No
	Democratic	Boston, Massachusetts	No	Yes
2000	Republican	Philadelphia, Pennsylvania	Yes	No
	Democratic	Los Angeles, California	Yes	Yes

* The 2020 conventions ended up being largely/entirely online due to Covid-19, but their locations had been chosen well in advance.

The Republican Convention: 'Trump Triumphant'

The 2024 Republican convention took place between 15–18 July in Milwaukee, Wisconsin. Over the course of four days, the Republicans ticked all the key boxes for a successful convention.

- Party unity ✔
- A range of slogans and straplines to energise the party faithful and, possibly, sway the uncommitted ✔
- Party platform endorsed ✔

- A range of speakers all praising Trump and the Republican cause ✔
- Absence of any major embarrassments or gaffes ✔
- A rousing end of convention speech by Trump ✔?
- A post-convention 'bounce' in the polls ✔

We now turn to look at each of these factors in a little more detail.

Party unity

The 2024 convention would be different from its two predecessors. Trump's dominance of the party was virtually complete. His primary opponents had swiftly fallen by the wayside, and the last woman standing, former UN Ambassador and South Carolina governor Nikki Haley, endorsed her rival saying, 'Donald Trump has my strong endorsement, period … You don't have to agree with Trump 100 percent of the time to vote for him.'

Add to that a clear lead in the polls, not least in the crucial battleground states such as Arizona and Georgia, and a visibly faltering Democrat incumbent in Joe Biden, then the path to the White House seemed clearcut. Furthermore, the assassination attempt on Trump just two days earlier, and little wonder this was a lovefest. Trump sported a bandage on the ear grazed by the shooter's bullet, and many of the audience sported a similar ear accessory in homage to his 'miraculous' survival! Even *The Guardian* newspaper, no supporter of Trump, admitted that the convention 'had the swagger of a party that believes it is on a glide path to the White House'.

Slogans and merch

Alongside all this, slogans were plentiful and on-message. Delegates brandished signs that included 'Make America Great Again', 'Trump = Success, Biden = Failure', 'Trump America First. Biden America Last', 'American oil from American soil' and 'Mass deportation now!' And most of these, and other statements of intent and policy, were also available as T-shirts, caps and coffee mugs. There was little similarity with the anger directed at Hillary Clinton in 2016. Gone for the most part were the petty and personal insults directed at Biden and Harris. Why after all go for the jugular when that ticket appeared half ripped up already? Instead, there was a positive pitch for a new, upgraded MAGA 2.0. Republicans were riding high anticipating four years in which to enact some bold policies with a Congress seemingly also to be controlled by the Republicans.

Party platform endorsed

The party platform had already been agreed by the party's top brass and above all by Trump, a week or so previously. Unlike 2020 when the 2016 platform was simply reissued, this was a new set of priorities. The overarching title was 'Make America Great Again'. Its less well-known dedication was 'To the Forgotten Men and Women of America', clear echoes perhaps of FDR's New Deal? We shall consider the parties' policies in more detail in Chapter 7.

A range of speakers

As with the Democratic convention, a large number of speakers were scheduled over the four days, with a clear pecking order in terms of times and day, all leading up to the main headline act who would close the show. Mostly, speakers comprised a range of Republican politicians, past and present including former House Speaker Newt Gingrich and current Speaker, Mike Johnson. Several former primary rivals of Trump also had a speaking slot including senators Ted Cruz and Tim Scott, and Florida governor Ron DeSantis. There was also a smattering of figures from the entertainment world including model, rapper and celebrity influencer Amber Rose and retired wrestler Hulk Hogan. TV host Tucker Carlson also spoke. Also, with Trump's personality and persona dominating the entire affair, there was room for several family members including daughter-in-law and RNC chair Lara Trump, his son Donald Trump Jr and his 17-year-old granddaughter, Kai Trump. Finally, Franklin Graham, son of the late and famous evangelist Billy Graham, also rallied the faithful.

What and who was missing

What is interesting is what was not in the list of policies and promises. Most conspicuous by its absence was anything substantial or specific on abortion. The policy statement had been culled from 775 words in 2020, to just 90. While there was a general commitment to protecting the right to life, the emphasis was on states' rights to decide legislation – a pragmatic concession to the political reality that the majority of Americans want abortion to be 'safe, legal and rare'. Aware that Democrats were keen to highlight women's reproductive rights as a key issue to rally their own voters, Trump preferred to avoid the issue beyond pointing to the reversal of *Roe v Wade* following his appointment of three pro-life justices to the Supreme Court.

There was also nothing on same sex marriage, again a policy area where there were few votes to be wooed. Although many Republicans, not least from the 'religious right', remain personally opposed to gay marriage, public opinion has shifted considerably rendering any mention of reversal or review a sure vote-loser.

The absence of certain individuals was also notable. Most prominent by his non-presence was Mike Pence, Trump's former VP and his running mate in 2020. The reason was not hard to fathom. Following his decision to certify the Electoral College votes in January 2021, many Republicans, not least Trump himself, saw him as a political Judas. As one Florida delegate put it, 'He betrayed his country'. There in person if not in spirit was then Republican Senate leader, Mitch McConnell. Having enjoyed, or more accurately endured, an icy relationship with Trump since the January 2021 Capitol riot, McConnell was not welcome. He was booed as he spoke on behalf of Kentucky's delegates during the roll call on the first day of the convention to formally nominate Donald Trump. Most poignantly perhaps, was the helmet and jacket of the firefighter Corey Comperatore who was killed by the sniper at the Trump rally in Pennsylvania where Trump had been shot at. Trump kissed the helmet as he paid an emotional tribute to the firefighter.

Absence of any major embarrassments or gaffes ... almost?
If by gaffes we mean the absence of any major missteps or unscripted moments, then the Republican convention passed off very smoothly. The only potential exception might have been Trump's rambling monologue/finale on the last day which lasted a record 92 minutes. It started off conventionally with reference to the assassination attempt. 'I stand before you in this arena only by the grace of Almighty God,' Trump intoned. There was a nod to unity and being a president for all Americans. And then it was 'Trump unfiltered'. The focus switched to familiar targets such as illegal migration, electric vehicles and the perils posed by the

Democrats in general not least to the economy, taxes and Medicare. Part of the rhetoric involved some unsubstantiated, or indeed incorrect, assertions and statistics. Among the less accurate statements were comments such as claiming 107% of jobs created under Biden were taken by illegal aliens, and the vivid image of immigrants 'coming from prisons, they're coming from jails, they're coming from mental institutions and insane asylums'.

So was this record-breaking acceptance speech a gaffe? Not in one sense. It gave his audience what they had come to hear, a man set aside to serve and save an America overrun with illegal immigrants, soaring crime and climate change fanaticism, from the clutches of dangerous/crazy Democrats. Perhaps then, not so much a gaffe as a missed opportunity to re-cast himself in a manner that was less adversarial and more reflective, one more likely to appeal to moderate and independent voters who actually decide elections in that handful of swing states. But like a salesman in love with his own product, Trump could not resist temptation with regard to his instincts, and nobody could tell him otherwise. But Trump's acceptance speech secured record viewing figures of over 28 million at its peak.

The verdict of the polls

While the final speech might have been unconventional or even a missed opportunity, the overall impact was favourable. The Republican convention had done its job well and Trump's poll ratings against Biden improved. Trump led Biden by six points (53% to 47%) in a 19–21 July survey taken just after the convention, a four-point increase in his lead over Biden since a 13–15 July poll taken immediately after the assassination attempt. But just when it seemed a slam dunk for the Republicans, the race became wide open again as Biden quit and anointed Harris to take over the Democratic nomination.

The Democratic Convention: 'Harris and her brat pack'

The political newsletter *The.Ink* authored by Anand Giridharadas, perhaps overdid it slightly when stating:

> The great political story of 2024 is President Biden's decision to stand aside in favour of Vice President Kamala Harris. It is a story of selflessness, of a generational transition in the rise of Harris, and of a woman who has at times struggled to command the narrative coming

into her own in a way that has energized the party and turned the race upside down.

But it is true that with Biden's exit, the race for the White House was transformed, yet again.

Unity

Initial fears over a divisive and thus damaging nomination process proved groundless. In a series of pre-convention deals and talks worthy of any 'smoke-filled room', successive potential challengers to Harris went public in announcing they were not seeking the presidential nomination. These included governors Gavin Newsom of California and Gretchen Whitmer of Michigan. It had helped that Biden had endorsed Harris from the start. Initially there seemed some desire for a competitive process to choose his successor. But within days of Biden's withdrawal, Team Harris had effectively sewn up the nomination process including endorsements from all 50 state Democratic Party chairs. Had their convention been a few weeks earlier, they might have struggled to wrap up their ticket in time.

When it came to the Gaza conflict, matters were trickier. Around 800,000 Democrat primary voters had voted 'uncommitted' in protest at the Biden administration's stance over the war in Gaza. Their demands were for an immediate ceasefire and an arms embargo on Israel. While Arab American influence and more widely that of a pro-Palestine sentiment has grown considerably in the Democrat Party in recent years, it still must contend with the power of the pro-Israel lobby and the powerful voice that Jewish Democrats and their supporters still hold within the party. An added complication perhaps, is that Harris's husband, Doug Emhoff, is the first ever Jewish spouse of a vice president and a leading campaigner against antisemitism.

The 30 or so 'uncommitted' Democrat delegates at the convention secured pledges from another 300-plus delegates to become ceasefire delegates. The group lobbied hard, but ultimately unsuccessfully, for a Palestinian speaker to be given a main stage speaking slot. This was despite the parents of an American-Israeli hostage of Hamas being given a slot. A number of the uncommitted delegates held an impromptu sit-in just outside the convention hall on the penultimate night. So, while major and open disunity on the main stage was avoided, the cause was not going anywhere soon. So, unity of sorts.

But if the main focus in Milwaukee was lauding Trump, a man who needed no introduction to friend or foe, the focus of the Democrat convention was subtly different. This was their make-or-break chance to repackage Harris as a presidential candidate with ideas of her own, not merely Biden's 'second stage of the rocket' for the second time. It was also a vital opportunity to present Harris's own running mate, Tim Walz, to the party faithful. With the title or slogan 'For the People, For Our Future', the Democratic Party wagon was ready to roll.

Party platform endorsed

The platform had largely been drafted before Biden's withdrawal and like its Republican counterpart was nuanced in places and bold elsewhere. It could be summarised as defending and championing the achievements of the Biden years, warning of the implications for democracy were Trump to be re-elected and laying out some policy promises for the next four years. The points below are again taken from the actual document and so need to be read with that important caveat.

Box 6.1 Extracts from the Democratic Party Platform, 2024

Policy boasts from the Biden–Harris administration included:
- We've created nearly 16 million jobs, a record number of small businesses are being started, and factories are coming home. We lowered families' health insurance premiums, and we stood up to Big Pharma to lower prescription drug prices.
- We're rebuilding our nation's roads, bridges, highways, ports, airports, water systems and more.
- We're seizing record amounts of fentanyl and securing our border in the face of Republican inaction. We're closing the racial wealth gap, and the gender pay gap.

Policy promises included:

- Strengthen enforcement and penalties for safety, wage, and other labour and employment violations.
- Continue to aggressively hold companies accountable for violating child labour law.
- Cut taxes for middle-class and low-income Americans and finance those cuts by making the ultra-wealthy and big corporations finally start paying their fair share.
- Keep pushing to reduce emissions from America's buildings and heavy industry. We support local and state efforts to adopt energy-efficient building codes. We'll require that low-carbon materials and clean power be used in all new federal buildings by 2030.
- Pass national legislation to make *Roe* the law of the land again. We will strengthen access to contraception so every woman who needs it is able to get and afford it. We will protect a woman's right to access IVF.
- Continue to fight for LGBTQI+ youth by building on President Biden's historic actions to ban so-called 'conversion therapy'; protecting LGBTQI+ children from bullying and discrimination; guaranteeing that transgender students are treated fairly and with respect at school.

Speakers

The speakers mirrored the Republicans in many ways, with Harris's speech the finale, and featured a range of speakers: past presidents (Bill Clinton and Barack Obama plus spouses), serving politicians including Chuck Schumer and Bernie Sanders, plus a couple of Republicans including former congressman Adam Kinzinger. It also had a hefty shot of Hollywood glitz including Stevie Wonder and Oprah Winfrey but not a rumoured surprise appearance from Beyoncé. 'Swifties' too would be disappointed. Ms Swift announced her endorsement of Harris only sometime after the convention. Joe Biden was given the primetime slot on the first day, very much in the manner of 'hail and farewell'.

Diversity was very much on parade, with the wide rainbow of the Democrat voting coalition present. Even those on the potentially disruptive left of the party were given a slot, including Alexandria Ocasio-Cortez (AOC). If lacking the family feel of the Trump show, there was nonetheless space on the speaker roster for Harris's husband, Doug Emhoff, and her sister Maya Harris.

A highlight in terms of the 'personal stories' was the introduction by the veteran civil rights activist Reverend Al Sharpton, of members of the exonerated Central Park Five – men of Black and Hispanic heritage who had been tried and convicted of a brutal rape in New York's Central Park back in 1989. They were later exonerated when a convicted rapist confessed to the crime, backed up by DNA evidence. The relevance of this was that Donald Trump, then a New York real estate developer, had taken out a full-page newspaper ad at the time calling for the return of the death penalty in New York State.

The headline act
While markedly shorter than Trump's speech, just 38 minutes, it nonetheless contained all the usual ingredients to rally the assembled crowd and display her vision for the nation if elected. There was a short section on her background and upbringing, 'They [her parents] instilled in us the values they personified – community, faith and the importance of treating others as you would want to be treated, with kindness, respect and compassion.' There was reference to her career as a lawyer: 'My entire career, I've only had one client – the people.' There were apocalyptic claims about a second-term Trump presidency:

> Just imagine Donald Trump with no guardrails, and how he would use the immense powers of the presidency of the United States, not to improve your life, not to strengthen our national security, but to serve the only client he has ever had – himself.

There were misleading statements about Trump wanting to ban abortion nationwide and limiting access to birth control. And, finally, there was the usual call to rally the troops:

> You know, our opponents in this race are out there every day denigrating America, talking about how terrible everything is. Well, my mother had another lesson she used to teach: Never let anyone tell you who you are. You show them who you are.

So, fewer digressions than Trump's end of convention speech, but still a clear desire to define herself, her values and to stoke fears about her opponent.

The verdict of the polls

The fairy dust of political conventions failed to weave its magic. Harris saw her popularity remain steady post-convention without much evidence of a 'bump'. That had occurred previously once she had emerged as Biden's successor, when a clear Trump lead had evaporated, and polls showed Harris leading by up to four percentage points. Here is evidence that conventions are there to be lost as well as won. The Harris campaign may not have benefitted from the 'Big Mo[mentum]' after Chicago, but it did them no disfavours. It was still 'Game On'.

CHAPTER 7

THE GENERAL ELECTION CAMPAIGN

Setting the scene

This was certainly an election campaign like no other in recent memory. For a start, it was a campaign devoid of its usual highlights – the three televised debates between the presidential candidates. This was the first time since 1996 that only two debates between the two major party candidates were scheduled. What is more, the final debate was held over two weeks before the date of the first debate in any of these other seven election cycles (see Table 7.1). This meant that for the last eight weeks of the campaign – between 11 September and 5 November – the only national event was the televised debate between the two running mates, Tim Walz and JD Vance, hardly a spectacle to get the heart racing. So if the campaign itself seemed somewhat featureless, it was because it was somewhat featureless.

Table 7.1 Dates of televised presidential debates, 1996–2024

Year	Democrat	Republican	1st Debate	2nd Debate	3rd Debate
1996	Bill Clinton	Bob Dole	6 Oct	16 Oct	-
2000	Al Gore	George W. Bush	3 Oct	11 Oct	17 Oct
2004	John Kerry	George W. Bush	30 Sept	8 Oct	13 Oct
2008	Barack Obama	John McCain	26 Sept	7 Oct	15 Oct
2012	Barack Obama	Mitt Romney	3 Oct	16 Oct	22 Oct
2016	Hillary Clinton	Donald Trump	26 Sept	9 Oct	19 Oct
2020	Joe Biden	Donald Trump	29 Sept	[15 Oct] †	22 Oct
2024	Kamala Harris	Donald Trump	27 Jun	10 Sep	-

† Debate cancelled because of Covid

The general election campaign – which traditional begins on Labor Day, the first Monday in September and runs for nine weeks – is played out almost exclusively in the media and in the 'swing states'. By 'swing states' we mean those states that might 'swing' either way – might be won by either party. In 2024, there were seven such swing states – Arizona, Georgia, Michigan, Nevada, North Carolina, Pennsylvania and Wisconsin. Unless you lived in one of these seven states, you would have seen very little, if anything, of the Trump–Harris race. This is one of the unintended consequences of the Electoral College system by which the president is elected. If the president were elected by the popular vote, then it would make sense to spend most of your time, energy and money in those states with the biggest population – California, Texas, Florida, New York and the like. But under the winner-takes-all system of the Electoral College, the Democrats know they will get more votes than the Republicans in California and New York, whilst the Republicans know they will get more votes than the Democrats in Texas and Florida. That's why neither Kamala Harris nor Donald Trump was concerned about running a very visible campaign in those states. And you can add another 39 states to that list – 17 of which are safe for the Democrats and 22 for the Republicans.

True, both parties would be keen to ensure that their likely voters in those 'safe states' were fired up and committed to turning out on Election Day. So, the Harris campaign would be using social media and TV ads to reach out to women, union members, suburban and younger voters and Black voters – groups of voters who typically vote Democrat – to try to ensure they would actually turn out on Election Day. Likewise, the Trump campaign would be reaching out to men, gun-owning rural voters, 'evangelical Christians' and older voters to fire them up to vote for Trump come 5 November.

The state of the race
So what was the state of the race at the start of September? By this time, Kamala Harris had been in the race for only six weeks. During the previous three months – from April to July – the polls had hardly moved at all. Donald Trump led Joe Biden throughout that period in the national head-to-head poll. Trump's numbers ranged from 44–47%; Biden's numbers from 43–46%. But now, in the six weeks since Biden had pulled out, the race had tightened. In the RealClearPolitics poll average, Harris was up from 44% to 48%; Trump was down from 48% to 46%. Since 5 August, Harris had been leading Trump in the national head-to-head poll.

But the movement in those seven swing states was even more dramatic. On the day when Biden pulled out of the race, Trump was leading in all those seven states by anything from two percentage points in Michigan to nearly seven percentage points in North Carolina. Now, on 1 September, Harris was leading in six of those states – albeit by a tiny margin – with Trump just hanging on to a small lead in North Carolina. As Table 7.2 shows, during these six weeks, all these seven states had swung to Harris by anything from 4 to 6.5 percentage points. But one must point out that all of Harris' leads were within the margin of error. Essentially, all the swing states were now tied. Biden's exit from the race had, at least for the time being, been a game-changer.

Table 7.2 Poll changes in swing states 21 July to 1 September

State	Leading in polls 21 July	Leading in polls 1 September	Swing
Arizona	Trump + 5.5	Harris + 0.2	Harris + 5.7
Georgia	Trump + 6.0	Harris + 0.4	Harris + 6.4
Michigan	Trump + 2.2	Harris + 2.4	Harris + 4.6
Nevada	Trump + 5.6	Harris + 0.8	Harris + 6.4
North Carolina	Trump + 6.9	Trump + 0.4	Harris + 6.5
Pennsylvania	Trump + 4.4	Harris + 1.2	Harris + 5.6
Wisconsin	Trump + 2.7	Harris + 3.2	Harris + 5.9

[Source: projects.fivethirtyeight.com/polls/]

This explains why Donald Trump appeared so frustrated – even angry – that he was no longer running against the 81-year-old incumbent president. Trump soon took to describing the Democrats' swapping Harris for Trump as a 'coup'. 'This was an overthrow of a president. This was an overthrow,' Trump said during a rally in Wilkes-Barre, a city in northeast Pennsylvania on 17 August. At the same event, Trump added: 'They deposed a president. It was a coup of a president. This was a coup.' It was, of course, nothing of the sort. But it was a useful line for Trump to spin in his preparation for a possible defeat in November. He would falsely claim – as he had done in 2020 – that the Democrats had cheated.

But Team Biden seemed to effortlessly morph into Team Harris. Biden's campaign chair Jen O'Malley Dillon was kept in post but told to hire top talent from the Clinton (2016) and Obama (2008 and 2012) presidential campaigns. Harris wanted them much more focused on polling. In terms of advertising, out would go the focus on 'defending democracy' and the portrayal of abstract 'American ideals' accompanied by lots of flag waving. The message was to be policy focused – the economy was now to be front and centre. Out went Biden's slogan 'Finish the Job'. In came her slogan 'A New Way Forward'. The new Harris rally chant, 'We're not going back' – an obvious reference to the Trump years – was to feature prominently. And certainly for those first six weeks, through late July and August, the Harris message began to bring a considerable uptick in the polls.

> **In the remainder of this chapter, we shall consider:**
> - The Harris–Trump TV debate
> - Campaign finance
> - Advertising
> - Policies
> - Campaigning in the swing states
> - Polling

The Harris–Trump TV debate

Never before had we seen a second televised presidential debate with a different candidate from the first debate! The Biden–Trump debate of June had become the Harris–Trump debate of September. By the time it came round, we realised that this would probably be the final consequential – potentially game-changing – event of the campaign. June had given us the first debate. July brought the assassination attempt on Trump, Biden's withdrawal from the race, and the Republican Convention. August brought the confirmation of the Harris–Walz ticket and the Democratic Convention. Now, in just the second week of September – with still eight weeks to go to Election Day – this seemed to be the last opportunity to shake up the race in any significant way.

In format, the second debate included the changes seen in the first debate – hosted by a TV network (this time ABC), with no audience, and the muting of microphones as an option if one candidate talked over the other. But the similarities ended there. From the very beginning, Kamala Harris was determined to make this a very different event. Whereas President Biden had shuffled somewhat uneasily onto the debate stage at the opening of the first debate ignoring Donald Trump, Vice President Harris strode on purposefully and immediately walked over to a somewhat surprised Donald Trump to shake his hand.

And the tone of the debate was different too. Harris was concise, focused and made her points with clarity. She laid out clearly the differences between her and her Republican opponent in terms of policies, character, experience and temperament. Trump, for his part, looked far less at ease than he had against Biden back in June. He also allowed himself to rise to Harris's bait to distract him onto his pet subjects such as the size of the crowds at his rallies and whether some attendees at these rallies left early. Indeed, it was the subject of Trump rallies that brought what was maybe the most memorable moment of the debate (see Box 7.1).

Box 7.1 Excerpt from Kamala Harris during TV debate

'I'm actually going to do something really unusual. I'm going to invite you to one of Donald Trump's rallies because it's a really interesting thing to watch. You will see during the course of his rallies he talks about fictional characters like Hannibal Lecter. He will talk about windmills cause cancer, and what you will notice is that people start leaving his rallies early out of exhaustion and boredom. And I will tell you, the one thing you will not hear him talk about is you. You will not hear him talk about your needs, your dreams and your desires. And you deserve a president who actually puts you first, and I pledge to you that I will.'

Another notable difference was that whereas Harris often turned to look over at Trump when she was talking about him, Trump stared straight ahead throughout the debate. Television also used the split-screen device so that one could see reactions whilst the other candidate was speaking. There were a number of times when Harris was seen contentedly smiling – even smirking – as Trump spoke, whilst Trump was seen scowling during Harris's interventions.

Table 7.3 Voting intentions of undecided swing state voters before/after debate

Voting intention	Before the debate	After the debate
Definitely Harris	0	5
Probably Harris	12	10
Neither	3	3
Probably Trump	10	6
Definitely Trump	0	0

During the debate, the *Washington Post* had a group of 25 uncommitted swing state voters watch the event, and then compared their voting intentions before and after the debate. The data in Table 7.3 show that these voters clearly swung more to Harris as a result of the debate. But the movement in the overall statewide and nationwide polls did not show such a marked bounce for Harris.

Campaign finance

That seemed all the more surprising when one considered that the Harris campaign raised much more money during these months than the Trump campaign as is shown in Figure 7.1. We need to divide this graph into two – the period from January through June during which time President Biden was the presumed Democratic Party candidate, and July through October when the candidate was Vice President Harris. During the first six months of 2024, the fundraising of the Biden and Trump campaigns was fairly even. Biden topped fundraising in four of those months; Trump topped it in two but very significantly in May raising almost twice as much as the Biden campaign. During these first six months, Harris raised $448 million to Trump's $424 million. Nothing much in it.

But then came President Biden's exit from the race on Sunday 21 July, and everything changed. 'Historic flood of cash pours into Harris campaign and allied groups,' headlined the *Washington Post* three days after Biden's exit from the race. Between that Sunday afternoon and the following Tuesday evening – in just two-and-a-half days – the Harris campaign reported raising $126 million from 1.4 million donors. Both figures are significant. The first for the sheer amount of money raised – equal to the amount raised for the entire month of June by the Biden campaign. The second because it shows that this was not just big dollar donations from a few very wealthy supporters. Campaigns love small donor contributions, not because they raise the most money – they clearly don't do that – but because they show individual commitment to the campaign, a commitment that will usually translate into votes. Data published on the Open Secrets website in late October, showed that the Harris campaign had raised 44% of all its money in contributions of less than $200. The figure for the Trump campaign was just 29%. 'If you give money to a candidate, you're probably going to make sure you go out and vote,' said Charles S. Bullock III, a political science professor at the University of Georgia.

Figure 7.1 Campaign fundraising by Biden/Harris† and Trump campaigns, Jan–Sept 2024 (millions of dollars)

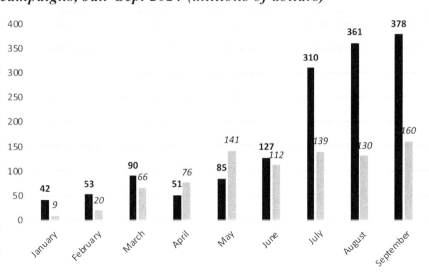

† Biden campaign (1 Jan–21 July); Harris campaign (22 July–30 Sept)

Furthermore, Table 7.4 shows how two significant events in the campaign – Biden's exit and the Harris–Trump TV debate – resulted in a huge disparity between the number of donors giving to the two campaigns. One would expect the first event to boost Harris rather than Trump, but the disparity on 10–11 September was more concerning for the Trump campaign.

In the first two full months of the Harris campaign – August and September – the data in Figure 7.1 show that Harris raised $739 million to Trump's $290 million, a remarkable turnaround from the first six months of the year. Not, of course, that more money necessarily turns into more votes. But more money does mean more money for campaign office staff in swing states, more money for Get Out the Vote (GOTV) operations across the country, more money for campaign ads on TV, billboards and social media, more money for rallies. At this stage in the campaign, the Harris campaign seemed to have stolen a significant advantage on Team Trump.

Table 7.4 Number of donors to the Harris and Trump campaigns on four given days

Date	Event	Number of donors to Harris campaign	Number of donors to Trump campaign
21 July	Biden exits race	604,000	7,000
22 July	Harris' first full day in race	651,000	7,000
10 Sept	Harris–Trump debate	486,000	14,000
11 Sept	Day after debate	344,000	12,000

[Source: 'Harris Leads Trump in Donors,' *Washington Post*, 23 October 2024]

Advertising

Designing and airing political commercials constitutes the main expense of contemporary presidential campaigns, expenses that have grown hugely since the turn of the millennium. Back in 2000, around $260 million was spent in that year's presidential campaign. By 2020, that figure had reached $1.5 billion. Veteran campaign scholar Professor Stephen Wayne sees three main factors responsible for this huge increase:

- The closeness of the races in all the elections.
- The passion of polarised partisan supporters.
- The proliferation of party and non-party groups.

All those factors were relevant in 2024.

Box 7.2 Scripts of three 2024 political ads

'Trump's project 2025 agenda will give him unchecked political power with no guardrails, and it would take Black Americans backwards. Project 2025 would strip away our voting rights protection and it eliminates the Department of Education. It would also require states to monitor women's pregnancies, it bans abortion, and would rip away health coverage from millions. Kamala Harris will stand up to Trump and his MAGA loyalist plans to control our lives. Because Trump is out for himself, while Kamala Harris is for the people.'

'With Kamala Harris we're seeing real change. She helped pass the Clean Energy Plan creating over 300,000 jobs and investing $32 billion into our communities and economy. But Donald Trump would take that all away. As president, Trump rolled back crucial environmental protections, sacrificing over a million clean energy jobs. He filled his administration with oil and gas lobbyists who put profit over people. Now Trump is asking for a billion-dollar bribe to kill clean energy jobs. We can't afford Donald Trump. The choice is clear. We are not going back. Vote Clean Energy.'

'This is America's border czar and she failed us. Under Harris, over 10 million illegally here, a quarter of a million Americans dead from fentanyl, brutal migrant crimes, and ISIS now here. Kamala Harris – Failed. Weak. Dangerously Liberal.'

In Box 7.2 are the scripts of three campaign ads from 2024. The first is a negative ad against Trump produced by the Harris campaign. This is aimed at linking Trump to 'Project 2025' – a 900-page wish list for the next Republican president published by the conservative think tank the Heritage Foundation. The second is another Harris ad which, although it opens as a positive ad about Harris's achievements, turns to negativity against what Trump would do if he were re-elected. It also contains one of Harris's oft-used slogans: 'We are not going back.' This is aimed at countering Trump's 'Make America Great Again' slogan and making it sound like an attempt to turn the clock back. Third, is a Trump ad criticising Harris's perceived policy failures regarding illegal immigration, drugs, crime and terrorism. It also uses one of Trump's oft-repeated slogans that Harris is 'dangerously liberal'.

Traditionally, political advertising was seen mostly in the United States on commercial television. But increasingly, campaigns have turned to social media to spread their messages. In 2024, the Harris campaign was much more focused on social media advertising than the Trump campaign. For example, in the week that included the only Trump–Harris TV debate on 10 September, Harris outspent Trump by 20 to 1 on Facebook and Instagram plastering the battleground states in a search for new voters and new donors. Harris spent $12.1 million on Meta's platforms during those days compared with Trump's just over $600,000. This fitted the trend of the campaign as a whole. The *Washington Post* reported the Harris campaign 'has overwhelmed the Trump operation with an avalanche of digital advertising, outspending his by tens of millions of dollars and setting off alarm among some Republicans'.

Back in 2020, the balance was the other way around with President Trump – awash with campaign funds – outspending the Democrats online. But this year, the *Post* reported, facing a cash shortfall, 'Mr. Trump is making a very different bet that emphasises the unique appeal of his broad online brand, and his belief in the power of television.' The Democrats were jubilant. 'It's a massive strategic advantage,' Kenneth Pennington, a Democratic digital strategist said of the Harris campaign's digital spending. 'And the Trump campaign just seems to be asleep at the wheel. Harris is running a more modern campaign.' With just weeks to go to Election Day, the Harris campaign had spent over $3 million on campaign ads on Snapchat. The Trump campaign had spent nothing. The Harris campaign seemed to be betting that she could reach critical voters in swing states on their phones and computers rather than relying simply on the conventional vehicles of rallies and television.

Policies

Gone are the days when it was quite hard to find significant policy differences between the two major parties. Certainly, the entrance of Donald Trump and the MAGA movement into national politics from 2016 has widened the policy gap between the Democrats and the Republicans. Table 7.5 compares the two candidates' policies in six key policy areas. In almost all these policy bullet points, the policies of one party are pretty much the direct opposite of the policies of the other. This is most clearly seen in such areas as abortion, climate and immigration. In Chapter 8, we shall see how these policies played out with the voters.

Table 7.5 Harris and Trump policies compared

Policy	Kamala Harris	Donald Trump
Abortion	• Supports legal access • Rejects efforts to limit access • Wants Congress to legislate to codify abortion rights	• Claims credit for Supreme Court overturning Roe v Wade • Wants the states to decide • Supports exceptions in cases of rape, incest and life of mother
Climate	• Agrees that climate change is caused by human activity and is an existential threat • Wants a blend of government action and market forces to combat global warming	• Claims that human activity is only one cause of climate change • Doesn't believe that climate change is making extreme weather events worse
Immigration	• Wants to revive the border compromise bill that Republicans refused to pass in 2024 • Sees family separation at the border as an abuse of human rights	• Proposes mass deportation of undocumented immigrants • Favours restoring family separations at the border • Proposes a travel ban from 'Muslim-majority countries'
Economy	• Supports raising taxes on corporations and high earners • Supports tax breaks for small business start-ups • Supports an increase in defence spending	• Supports tax cuts for corporations and high earners • As president, Trump signed the largest defence budget ever, but has accused Biden of spending too much on defence

Foreign policy	• Regards China as a threat to the US • Promises to support Ukraine in its war against Russia • Committed to honouring obligations to Taiwan • Wants an immediate ceasefire in Gaza	• Claims that he can negotiate with China and Russia • Wants support for Ukraine to be 'conditional'; claims he could bring about an end to the war • Unclear on both Taiwan and Gaza
Crime & guns	• Supports criminal justice reform • Supports laws to restrict gun ownership for those who might harm themselves or others • Supports gun manufacturers being sued in court • She owns a gun	• Supports criminal justice reform • Opposes restricting access to guns for those who might harm themselves or others • Opposes gun manufacturers being sued in court • He owns guns

Throughout her campaign, Kamala Harris stuck closely to the Biden agenda, a possible error of judgement, the significance of which would not become fully clear until the results started to roll in on election night and the data from exit polls analysed. Appearing on ABC's *The View* in early October, host Sunny Hostin asked the Vice President: 'What if anything would you have done differently than President Biden during the past four years?' Harris answered without hesitation: 'There's not a thing that comes to mind.' It wasn't an answer that sat easily with her claim to be the candidate of change, the one to 'turn the page'. Neither did it make much electoral sense to attach herself so closely to a president whose approval ratings were below 40%.

Campaigning in the swing states

After the Harris–Trump TV debate in Philadelphia on 10 September, Donald Trump and Kamala Harris – along with their respective running mates – set off for the swing states, the battleground of the eight-week general election campaign. Kamala Harris stayed to campaign in Pennsylvania. By this stage, most commentators had concluded that whichever candidate won Pennsylvania would win the election. Trump had won it by just 40,000 votes back in 2016 – out of over 6 million votes cast statewide. Biden had won it by around 80,000 votes in 2020 – out of nearly 7 million. Five of Harris's first eight rallies in September were held in the state.

Donald Trump had a more leisurely start to his campaign in September. In those first 17 days of the month during which Kamala Harris was clocking up eight rallies, Trump held just three – one each in Wisconsin, Arizona and Nevada, all states that Trump had narrowly lost in 2020. But as September morphed into October and Election Day began to loom over the horizon, both candidates pulled out all the stops in terms of rallies in the swing states. Table 7.6 shows the number of rallies that Kamala Harris and Donald Trump held in these seven states during the three months leading up to Election Day.

Table 7.6 Number of rallies held by Harris and Trump in the swing states, 6 August–4 November

State	Kamala Harris	Donald Trump
Arizona	5	4
Georgia	8	7
Michigan	15	8
Nevada	4	4
North Carolina	6	11
Pennsylvania	18	15
Wisconsin	12	6
TOTAL	68	55

We can see from this data that both candidates focused more attention on Pennsylvania than any other state. We can also see that in addition, Harris focused more on the 'blue wall' or old Rust Belt states of Pennsylvania, Michigan and Wisconsin, holding 45 events in just those three states during the last three months of the campaign. But she made fewer visits to the Sun Belt states of Arizona, Georgia, North Carolina and Nevada. Trump concentrated on Pennsylvania too with 15 events, but also North Carolina – a state he won both in 2016 and 2020, even campaigning there again on the very eve of the election suggesting that his team were still not certain that he could be confident of the result there.

There was a further significant difference between the two campaigns. Harris held only three rallies outside these seven states during this period – including one on The Ellipse in Washington DC in late October, the same spot as Donald Trump had held his rally on 6 January 2021, before the storming of the Capitol by his supporters. Trump, on the other hand, held rallies in Montana, Colorado, California, Florida, New Mexico and Virginia as well as two in New York – including one in Madison Square Garden in late October.

But one needs to keep in mind these days that almost all states allow early voting. Indeed, voting was taking place in 12 states even by the end of September (see Figure 7.2). So events that occur in the final days of the campaign maybe don't have the importance that they used to have, say, two decades ago.

Figure 7.2 Cumulative number of states allowing early voting by given date, 2024

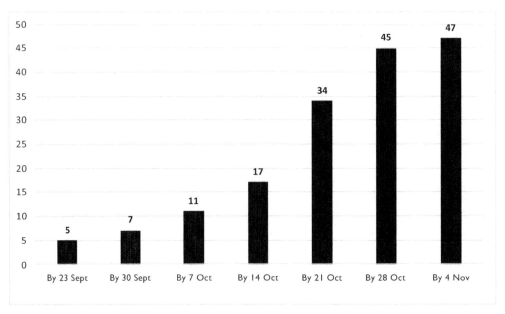

Polling

This election campaign was noteworthy for the fact that the polls shifted so little throughout it. The only event that significantly moved the polls was Joe Biden's withdrawal from the race and Kamala Harris' entry. As Table 7.2 opposite has shown, as soon as Harris entered the race the Democrats' standing in the race improved significantly in the swing states. But nothing else really 'moved the needle' as we say, but the race did tighten as Election Day approached. Whereas Harris had led in some swing states by two or three points in early September, those leads had dwindled as Election Day neared. Was there an uptick for Harris in the final days or hours of the campaign? Some were suggesting so. And a poll showing Harris leading Trump by three percentage points in the midwestern state of Iowa which Trump had won by eight points in 2020 certainly caused a flutter of excitement in the Harris camp. All the media were reporting that the polls made the election 'too close to call'. But would the polls be right?

CHAPTER 8
WHO WON, AND WHY

At 5.31am Eastern Standard Time on the morning of Wednesday 6 November – less than nine hours after the polls had closed on America's west coast – CNN called the presidential election for Donald Trump. So much for a close race, the result of which wouldn't be known for days. And so much for the expectation of America's first woman president. For the second time in eight years the Democratic Party's female presidential candidate had lost – and to the same Republican male candidate. Donald Trump became the first person to win back the presidential office he had lost four years earlier since Grover Cleveland in 1892 (see Chapter 1). In winning back the White House for the Republicans, Trump not only held on to North Carolina – a state he had won back in 2020 by a whisker – but added all the other swing states. He won in the Rust Belt (Pennsylvania, Wisconsin and Michigan) and in the Sun Belt (Georgia, Arizona and Nevada). He also became the first Republican presidential candidate to win the popular vote since George W. Bush was re-elected in 2004. Trump won in an electorate that was whiter and significantly older than in 2020, and one in which turnout was down. When Trump won in 2016, over 65s made up just 15% of voters. By 2020, that had increased to 22% and by 2024 to 28%. The combined vote for the two major parties in 2020 was around 156 million. In 2024 it was nearer 152 million. In the Electoral College, Trump won by 312 votes to 226 – the most electoral college votes for a Republican since George H.W. Bush won 426 votes in 1988. So, why did Trump win?

In this chapter, we shall consider six major – and to some extent interrelated – reasons why Trump won:
1. The economy
2. Illegal immigration
3. The 'Radical Left' label stuck to Harris
4. Trump won new voters
5. The abortion issue didn't work for Harris
6. Biden's late exit

I.   The economy

Back in 1992 when Democrat Bill Clinton was facing Republican president George H.W. Bush, one of his closest aides, James Carville, famously posted a list of what he thought should be the Clinton campaign's top three priorities. It read:

1.   Change vs more of the same

2.   The economy, stupid!

3.   Don't forget health care.

The second priority became popularised in the phrase, 'It's the economy, stupid!' It was almost as if Donald Trump had adopted it as his campaign slogan in 2024. Time and again as we dig deeper into the exit poll data, we find that it was voters' view of the economy, and which of the two candidates they thought was most likely to best handle the economy, that was the crucial factor in deciding people's votes, and the outcome of the election.

Table 8.1 shows the answers to the question, 'How would you describe the condition of the nation's economy – excellent, good, not so good or poor?' Just 5% of voters described the US economy as 'excellent' and only 27% as 'good'. True, Harris got the votes of around 90% of those voters, but they made up only one-third of the electorate. The other two-thirds described America's economy as 'not so good' (35%) or 'poor' (33%), and they overwhelmingly voted for Trump. Of the one-third of voters who described the economy as 'poor', Trump won just shy of nine out of every ten votes. That in itself is a very difficult margin to overcome – whatever voters might think about safeguarding democracy, a woman's right to choose, or Trump's multiple criminal cases.

Table 8.1

Condition of the nation's economy	Trump (%)	Harris (%)
Excellent (5%)	10	89
Good (27%)	8	91
Not so good (35%)	54	44
Poor (33%)	87	10

But Vice President Harris had been telling Americans that the economy was now flourishing. It wasn't so much that they didn't believe her, as they hadn't yet seen the evidence for that in their personal budgets – at the grocery store, at the gas station. Voters were not just thinking about the economy in November 2024 but over the whole four-year period of the Biden–Harris administration. It was therefore canny campaigning when Donald Trump posed the same question that Ronald Reagan had posed in 1980 when he was running against President Carter: 'Are you better off than you were four years ago?' Trump, like Reagan, knew that most voters would answer in the negative.

Figure 8.1 Average annual inflation in consumer prices by administration: Ford to Biden

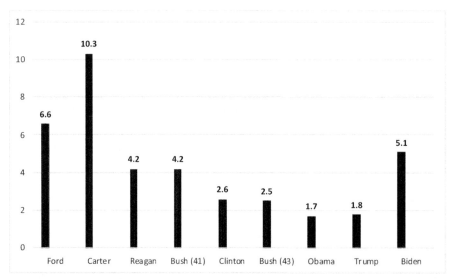

[Source: Bureau of Labour Statistics]

Figure 8.1 shows the average annual inflation during the last nine administrations. Two things stand out from this graph. First, that the average annual inflation rate of 5.1% during the Biden–Harris administration had been the highest for over 40 years – since the 10.3% during the Carter years in the late 1970s. Second, it shows clearly why so many voters were saying that they thought they were better off under Donald Trump in his first term. Quite simply, they were right. They had been – a lot better off. True, Biden and Harris could point out the cost and consequences of the Covid pandemic. But that just didn't resonate with so many voters.

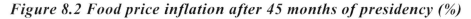

Figure 8.2 Food price inflation after 45 months of presidency (%)

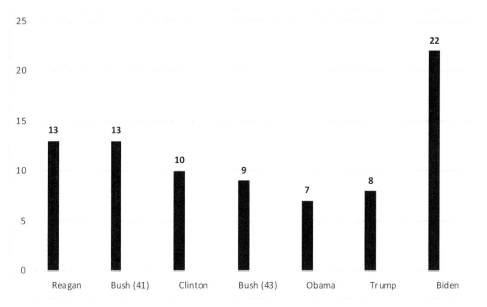

This feeling of having been better off under Trump was further reinforced when one considers food price inflation. Figure 8.2 shows the percentage food price inflation after 45 months of each presidency going back to October 1984 and President Reagan. Again, this graph shows the same two trends. Not only was food price inflation under Biden much higher than under any previous administration in the past 40 years, but it was significantly higher than under Donald Trump in 2020. Whereas food prices had risen 8% in the period between January 2017 and October 2020 under Trump, they had risen 22% in the period between January 2021 and October 2024 under Biden–Harris. Maybe the crucial factor was not so much 'the economy' as 'affordability'.

Table 8.2

In past year, inflation has caused your family:	Trump (%)	Harris (%)
Severe hardship (22%)	74	24
Moderate hardship (53%)	51	45
No hardship (24%)	20	77

Exit poll data shows that nearly one quarter of voters said that inflation had caused 'severe hardship' in their family in the past year (see Table 8.2).

Of those, 74% voted for Trump. Trump also won the majority of the votes of those who described such hardship caused by inflation as 'moderate' winning that group by 7 points over Harris. As Megan McArdle wrote in the *Washington Post* the day after the election: 'The clearest message of this election is that people really, really, really hate inflation … You will get unearned credit if the economy booms and unearned blame if it craters. Some of that blame rubbed off on Harris:'

Table 8.3 Who voted for whom

Category	2020		2024		% point change for R since 2020
	Trump (R) (%)	Biden (D) (%)	Trump (R) (%)	Harris (D) (%)	
All (100)	47	51	50	48	+3
Men (47)	53	45	55	42	+2
Women (53)	42	57	45	53	+3
White (71)	58	41	57	41	-1
Black (11)	12	87	13	85	+1
Latino (12)	32	65	46	52	+14
Asian (3)	34	61	39	54	+5
White men (34)	61	38	60	37	-1
White women (37)	55	44	53	45	-2
Black men (5)	19	79	21	77	+2
Black women (7)	9	90	7	91	-2
Latino men (6)	36	59	55	43	+19
Latina women (6)	30	69	38	60	+8
White 18–29 (8)	53	44	49	49	-4
White 30–44 (15)	57	41	55	42	-2
White 45–64 (25)	61	32	62	37	+1
White 65+ (22)	57	44	55	44	-2
Aged 18–29 (14)	36	60	43	54	+7
Aged 30–44 (23)	46	52	48	49	+2
Aged 45–64 (35)	50	49	54	44	+4
Aged 65+ (28)	52	47	49	49	-3
Protestant (42)	60	39	63	36	+3
White evangelical (22)	76	24	82	17	+6
Catholic (22)	47	52	58	40	+11

Never attended college (57)	50	48	**56**	42	+6
College graduate (43)	43	55	42	**55**	-1
White non-college (39)	67	32	**66**	32	-1
White non-coll. men (18)	70	28	**69**	29	-1
White non-coll. women (20)	63	36	**63**	35	0
White college grad (33)	48	51	45	52	-3
White coll. grad men (16)	51	48	**50**	47	-1
White coll. grad women (17)	45	54	41	57	-4
Urban (29)	38	60	38	**59**	0
Suburban (51)	48	50	**51**	47	+3
Rural (19)	57	42	**64**	34	+7
Democrats (31)	5	94	4	**95**	-1
Republicans (35)	94	6	**94**	5	0
Independents (34)	41	54	46	**49**	+5
Liberal (23)	10	89	7	**91**	-3
Moderate (42)	34	64	40	**57**	+6
Conservatives (34)	85	14	**90**	9	+5
Family income:					
Under $50,000 (27)	44	55	**50**	47	+6
$50–99,999 (33)	42	57	**49**	47	+7
$100,000 and over (40)	54	42	46	**51**	-8

Box 8.1

"The clearest message of this election is that people really, really, really hate inflation, and they punish incumbents who preside over it. Democrats might justly protest that this is unfair – while Biden did gobs of inflationary deficit spending, so did Trump, and the President certainly didn't cause the pandemic-induced supply-chain bottlenecks that caused prices to rise worldwide. But that's the risk you take when running for the office: You will get unearned credit if the economy booms, and unearned blame if it craters. Some of that blame rubbed off on Harris."

Megan McArdle, 'Don't Lose Sight of Why Trump Won,' *Washington Post*, 6 November, 2024.

To compound these bad economic facts and figures for Harris, voters believed – probably based on memories from just four years ago – that Trump (52%) would handle the economy better than Harris (46%). The economy under the Biden–Harris administration was the most significant factor in deciding the result of the election. As Brian Riedl, senior fellow at the Manhattan Institute, a centre-right think tank, commented: 'It's hard for your party to hold the White House when the inflation rate hits 9% under your watch.'

So whilst first Biden and then Harris were (correctly) telling Americans that the US economy was, in the words of *The Economist*, 'the envy of the world,' what this election showed is that for ordinary voters – and especially for the less well-off – anger about prices trumps macroeconomic analysis.

2.   Illegal immigration

Three days after the election, Fareed Zakaria wrote an article for the *Washington Post* entitled 'Democrats' Three Big Mistakes' in which he stated:

> The first big error was the Biden administration's blindness to the collapse of the immigration system and the chaos at the border. An asylum system that was meant for a small number of persecuted individuals was being used by millions to gain legal entry. Instead of shutting it down, liberals branded anyone protesting as heartless and racist.

Kamala Harris, along with the vast majority of Democrats, had missed a massive shift in American public opinion that had occurred in just a few years. In 2020, the percentage of Americans who wanted to decrease immigration was 28%; by this year, it was 55%. When Harris went on ABC's 'The View' just a month before Election Day and was asked how she would have differed from Biden, instead of basically saying she wouldn't have done anything differently (see Chapter 7), what she should have said was, 'I would have shut down the border early and hard.'

Donald Trump's victory on 5 November 2024, clearly showed that illegal immigration is very unpopular, and that the positions Kamala Harris and the Democrats took were further to the left than the American public is comfortable with. It remains to be seen how much genuine support there will be for the 'mass deportations' of illegal immigrants of which Trump spoke frequently in his campaign rallies – or even whether such a policy is judicially and executively feasible – but clearly Trump and the Republicans were more in tune with the majority of Americans on this issue than Harris and the Democrats.

Didi Martinez, a reporter for NBC News, quoted 60-year-old mechanic Michael Perez from the swing state of Pennsylvania who said that immigration was his top concern. 'The border. Shut it down,' he said, pointing to media reports about the presence of the Venezuelan gang Tren de Aragua in several US communities. In the September NBC News poll, Trump had a lead over Harris among Latino voters on the economy, inflation and securing the border.

In the final days of her campaign, Kamala Harris had reverted to Biden's lines about Trump's perceived unsuitability for office and the threat he supposedly posed to the country's democratic norms and institutions. Those were not the issues that were going to sway the minds of undecided voters in the swing states. They were focused on the economy and illegal immigration, and only Donald Trump was addressing those issues.

Of the 11% of voters who said that immigration was the most important issue in the campaign, nine out of every ten voted for Donald Trump. What is more, by a 9-point margin (53–44), voters said they could trust Trump more than Harris to handle the question of illegal immigration.

3.   The 'Radical Left' label stuck to Harris

Addressing a huge rally in New York's Madison Square Garden in October, Donald Trump repeated a line of attack that he had used throughout the campaign, describing Kamala Harris as 'a radical left lunatic who destroyed California'. (Harris had been the state's Attorney General before being elected to represent the state in the United States Senate.) 'Radical left-wing extremist', 'communist', 'Marxist', were all labels that Trump frequently used to describe his opponent. The labels – though not entirely true – stuck. How did that happen?

It's a rule of negative political campaigning that it works only when people recognise the negative characteristic as being partly true. So when the Democrats in 1980 tried to paint Ronald Reagan as a dangerous extremist it didn't work because it didn't square with what voters already knew and believed about Reagan. The trouble for Kamala Harris in 2024 was that there was enough recognisable truth in the 'leftist' accusations against her that people were more willing to believe the exaggerations.

Table 8.4 Favourable/unfavourable views of Trump and Harris

What is your view of:	Favourable (%)	Unfavourable (%)
Donald Trump	46	53
Kamala Harris	47	52

Table 8.5 Are Trump's/Harris's views too extreme?

Are their views too extreme?	Yes (%)	No (%)
Donald Trump	54	44
Kamala Harris	47	50

For a start, Harris came from California. Voters in the centre and on the right of politics in the US tend to see 'California' as a synonym for 'liberal', even far-left liberal. Joe Biden had been raised in Pennsylvania and then lived a lifetime in the east coast state of Delaware. Neither of those states is linked in Americans' minds with being a hotbed of liberalism.

Second, her four-year voting record in the Senate was the voting record of a liberal Democrat. In the 115th Congress (2017–19), 48 Democrats served in the Senate. Of those 48, Harris had the third-most liberal voting record. Only Elizabeth Warren of Massachusetts and Kirsten Gillibrand of New York had a higher liberal voting score. In the 116th Congress (2019–21) Harris had the second-most liberal voting record of the 45 Democrats who served. If we broaden that out and look at all the 109 Democrats who had served in the Senate this century, Harris had the second-most liberal voting record. Comparing that with the other three Democratic presidential candidates of this century who have served in the Senate, Hillary Clinton comes it at 35th, Barack Obama at 47th and Joe Biden at 57th. So Joe Biden at 57/109 puts him in the ideological centre of the modern Democratic Party. Harris, unlike Biden, was not a Senate centrist. That's why the label stuck.

Third, when Harris ran for the presidential nomination of her party against Biden and others in 2020, she ran a campaign from the left of the party. She said she opposed fracking, would 'think about' abolishing the Immigration and Customs Enforcement Agency, called the idea of adding more police officers 'wrongheaded thinking', said she was considering the idea of letting convicted federal criminals vote, supported a 'mandatory buyback programme' for some guns and called for the elimination of private health insurance. The Trump campaign's TV ads were full of extracts of such statements (see Box 8.2).

Box 8.2

'The archive is deep. We will run out of time before we run out of video clips of Kamala Harris saying wacky California liberal things. I'm just not sure that the rest of this campaign includes much besides that.'

David McCormick, a Republican election strategist. Extract from Reid Epstein, 'Why the Kamala Harris of Four Years Ago Could Haunt Her in 2024,' *New York Times*, 29 July 2024.

This goes some way to explain Harris's high unfavourable figure (52%) – only one percentage point lower than Trump's (see Table 8.4). And whilst 54% of voters told exit polls they thought Donald Trump was 'too extreme', 47% described Kamala Harris the same way (see Table 8.5). Trump's labels of Harris stuck.

4.   Trump won new voters

For the first time in 20 years, a Republican presidential candidate won the popular vote. After each of the past four elections we've been saying that the Republicans lost the popular vote because they failed to grow their pool of voters. They played only to their party base. As one watched the 2024 campaign, it looked as if they were making the same mistake again. But the results and the exit polls showed that this was not the case. The Republicans grew their pool of supporters in some significant ways.

Latino voters

Of all the voting groups listed in Table 8.3 above, it's the change amongst Latino voters, and especially amongst Latino men, that is the real stand-out. As recently as 2012, Latino voters gave just 27% of their votes to

Republican candidate Mitt Romney. Even more remarkably, in 2016, Donald Trump picked up just 29% of the Latino vote. Two elections later in 2024, Trump won 46% of the Latino vote and 55% of the vote amongst Latino men, the latter share being up 19 percentage points from 2020! With Latino voters for the first time being more numerous that Black voters, this was critical to Trump's victory. As Table 8.6 shows, the Democrats had gone from having a +44-point margin amongst Latino voters in 2012 to a mere +6-point margin in the space of just three elections.

Yet Donald Trump had called Latino migrants rapists, murderers and drug dealers. In one of his final rallies of his campaign, a comedian on stage described Puerto Rico as 'a floating island of garbage'. Many commentators and election-watchers – including this author – thought Latinos would decisively turn against the Republican ticket. We were wrong. So how could Latinos – many of whose family members could be targeted by any mass deportations promised by Donald Trump – make the choice to support the Trump–Vance ticket in such huge numbers? There are three possible ways of answering that, all of which relate back to the issues we have already discussed – the economy, illegal immigration and the perceived leftist stance of Kamala Harris.

Table 8.6 Latino vote by party in presidential elections: 2008–24

Year	Republican candidate	Democratic vote by Latinos (%)	Republican vote by Latinos (%)	Margin
2008	John McCain	67	31	D +36
2012	Mitt Romney	71	27	D +44
2016	Donald Trump	65	29	D +36
2020	Donald Trump	65	32	D +33
2024	Donald Trump	52	46	D +6

Writing in *The Atlantic* magazine straight after the election, Xochitl Gonzalez – whose father was a Puerto Rican veteran of World War Two – stated:

Latinos broke for Trump for many complicated reasons, including sexism, religious conservatism, racism (or a desire to assimilate into whiteness). But the simplest answer is often the best: To many, Trump represents prosperity. And the ability to financially prosper is what America is all about.

> ## Why did so many Latino voters move to the Republicans in 2024?
> 1. The economy
> 2. Illegal immigration
> 3. Faith and values

In polls, Latinos consistently put economic issues at the top of their list of concerns. After the election, the media was full of voters reaffirming this. One Pennsylvania voter of Puerto Rican descent told NBC News he wasn't bothered by Trump's comments about the island: 'For me, it's work. It's the economy. It's groceries.' So reason number one for the movement of Latino voters to the Republicans in 2024 was, again, the economy.

But there were also those in the Latino community who, having come to America, waited their turn and settled legally, resented those 'illegals' streaming across the Mexican border – almost as much as, if not more than, those white voters who made up the largest part of Trump's base. They, too, wanted a strong border. So the second reason harks back to illegal immigration.

The third reason has to do with faith and values. Interviewed on the *PBS NewsHour* a week after the election, the Reverend Samuel Rodriguez of the National Hispanic Christian Leadership Conference told interviewer Geoff Bennett:

> The primary reason has to do with faith. Latinos are becoming more and more evangelical every single year. So Latinos are becoming more conservative because of their faith.

He also harked back to what he saw as the leftward movement in the Democratic Party, claiming that the Democratic Party was now no longer the party of 2008 and Barack Obama. So putting those two things together, the policies of Donald Trump's Republican Party looked very attractive. He said it was a matter of balancing a Harris administration 'coming and intruding on the way I raise my children' and 'the character, rhetoric, tweets and bravado' of Donald Trump. So, Rodriguez and many Latinos concluded about Trump: 'We don't like the guy, but his policies were amazing and his policies lined up with what we believe.' As for Harris and the Democrats: 'The Party sounds good but their policies are counterintuitive to who I am as a Latino and as a Christian.'

Catholic voters

In previous elections we have talked a lot about white 'evangelical' voters and their solid support for Donald Trump. That trend continued in 2024. But the really big story regarding the voting of religious groups was the 11 percentage point increase in the Catholic vote for Trump as compared with 2020. Trump's 58% from Catholic voters was the highest for a Republican presidential candidate since the 59% of Catholics who voted for George H.W. Bush in 1988 (see Figure 8.3).

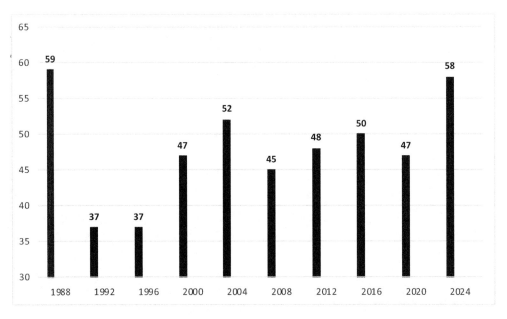

Indeed, in nine of the last ten elections, Catholics have given the majority of their votes to the winning candidate – the only exception being 2000 when they narrowly went for Democrat Al Gore over Republican George W. Bush, but then Gore did win the popular vote that year.

According to Tyler Arnold writing in the Catholic journal *The Tablet*, both Trump and his running mate JD Vance courted the Catholic vote heavily in the final weeks of the campaign. In late October, Trump called Harris 'destructive to Christianity' and said that Catholics were being 'treated worse than anybody'. In the crucial swing state of Pennsylvania, Vance wrote an op-ed piece for the *Pittsburgh Post-Gazette* in which he accused Harris of 'prejudice against Catholics'. Given the Catholic church's conservative teaching on abortion, here was another example of a group of voters voting in line with their faith and their values.

The 12 percentage-point fall in the Catholic vote for the Democrats – from 52% for Biden in 2020 to 40% for Harris in 2024 – reflected the fact that Joe Biden was someone who was very open about his being a devout Catholic. Harris, on the other hand, is a member of a Baptist Church in San Francisco – a church closely associated with the Black civil rights movement, hardly a point of attraction for wavering Republicans.

In a race that in the end would come down to around 2 percentage points in the popular vote, the loss of so many voters in a group that accounted for nearly one-quarter of all voters was highly significant.

Black men

This represented the fourth consecutive election which saw an increase in the percentage of Black men voting for the Republican presidential candidate. Back in 2008, the Democrats – with their first Black presidential candidate – received 95% of the vote from Black men. The Republican, John McCain, got just 5%. By 2024, the Democrats – with their second Black presidential candidate – received 77% of the vote from Black men. Donald Trump won 21%.

Box 8.3 Extract from 'How Trump Won and How Harris Lost', by Shane Goldmacher, New York Times 7 November

'Mr Trump's approach to gender could not have been more different from Ms. Harris's. His team's data clearly showed that the highest return on investment would be a group that didn't often vote: younger men, including Hispanic and Black men who were struggling with inflation, alienated by left-wing ideology and pessimistic about the country.'

In two of the swing states – North Carolina and Pennsylvania – Trump's support amongst Black men was up significantly from 2020. In North Carolina it was up 13 percentage points, from 8% to 21%; in Pennsylvania it was up 16 percentage points, from 10% to 26%. In Pennsylvania, there was also an extraordinary difference between the way Black men and Black women voted. Whilst 26% of Black men voted for Trump, just 3% of Black women voted for him. The executive director of the non-partisan group Black Men Vote told the CBS affiliate TV station in Philadelphia the weekend before Election Day that 'we will be the difference-makers in this election'. They might well have been, but not in the way most would have expected.

Young voters
Table 8.3 also shows that Donald Trump significantly improved his vote share amongst young (18–29-year-olds) voters, up from 36% in 2020 to 43% in 2024. But as Table 8.7 shows, in some of the crucial swing states, Trump's performance amongst these voters was even more impressive, especially in Michigan, North Carolina, Pennsylvania and Wisconsin.

Table 8.7 Republican vote amongst 18–29-year-olds, 2020 and 2024 compared

State	Republican vote amongst 18–29-year-olds in 2020	Republican vote amongst 18–29-year-olds in 2024	Change from 2020 to 2024
Arizona	32%	34%	+2
Georgia	43%	38%	-5
Michigan	37%	49%	+12
Nevada	33%	38%	+5
North Carolina	40%	48%	+8
Pennsylvania	35%	44%	+9
Wisconsin	36%	45%	+9

The Trump campaign committed its limited resources and Trump's time to communicating with young voters – especially young men. Trump spent little time doing mainstream media interviews and instead recorded a series of podcast interviews which tapped into younger audiences.

Non-college educated voters

The final group amongst which Trump significantly improved his support was amongst those voters who had never gone to college – that is those who had no full-time education after leaving high school aged 18. In 2020, they had split 50-48 for Trump, but in 2024 they split 56-42 for Trump – a two-point lead for Trump turning into a 14-point lead for Trump. As E.J. Dionne wrote in the *Washington Post* just after the election ('Did You Miss the Trump Surge?'):

> It shouldn't keep surprising us that Americans without college degrees are still upset after four decades of economic change imposing its heaviest burdens on them. The outcome will be a bitter irony for Biden, since much of his programme was directed to help those left behind, and real wages after inflation rose most in the Biden years for the lowest-income workers.

Conclusion

Thus Trump's Republicans did what they had not managed to do for some two decades – to build a winning coalition of white men, white evangelicals, Catholics, Black men, Latinos, young voters, and those without a college education. That's more a mosaic than a monolith. Now the challenge will be to keep that mosaic from fracturing into disparate pieces in four years' time.

5.   The abortion issue didn't work for Harris

One thing we learnt on 5 November – 2024 was not 2022. In the midterm elections in 2022, the Democrats did much better than they were expecting mainly because of the support they got as a reaction of women who were both worried and angry at the Supreme Court's decision in *Dobbs v Jackson Women's Health Organization* which overturned the *Roe v Wade* decision 50 years earlier. In 2024, with a woman at the top of their national ticket, Democrats played the Dobbs card again. At rally after rally, Kamala Harris spoke of 'a woman's right to choose' and 'to make decisions for her own body'. And with what result? The Democrats' vote amongst women fell by 4 percentage points – from 57% to 53%. Indeed, as Table 8.8 shows, this was the Democrats' worst result amongst women voters for two decades!

Table 8.8 Democrats' lead amongst women voters, 2004–24

Year	Women voting D (%)	Women voting R (%)	D lead amongst women voters
2004	51	48	+3
2008	56	43	+13
2012	55	44	+11
2016	54	42	+12
2020	57	42	+15
2024	53	45	+8

In four of the swing states, the women's vote for Harris was down on what it had been for Biden in 2020. A 14-point margin for Biden amongst women in Michigan in 2020 turned into just a 9-point margin amongst women in Michigan in 2024. In Arizona, Trump got more votes from women voters than Harris!

Not only did the abortion issue not work for Harris amongst women, there seems to be evidence that the stress on a pro-choice agenda put off some groups of voters – especially Latinos.

6. Biden's late exit

In the days immediately after the election result was known, much commentary focused on this particular factor. Some seemed to be implying that if only President Biden hadn't run for re-election, the Democrats would have won – easily. But that's a simplistic argument for which there is little evidence. But that's not to say that Joe Biden wasn't a factor at all in this election. But notice we've placed him sixth!

Whilst running in the Democratic primaries in March 2020, Biden – already 77 years old – stated, 'Look, I view myself as a bridge, not as anything else. There's an entire generation of leaders … They are the future of this country.' Most interpreted that as Biden's promise that if elected he would serve only one term. But, convinced that only he could defeat Donald Trump in 2024, Biden headed into a re-election campaign with hardly a murmur of dissent from the party's hierarchy. It wasn't until his disastrous performance in the TV debate with Trump in late June that Biden was faced with a barrage of criticism from within his own party and calls for him to step aside.

But by the time that decision was taken – in late July – there was really no option for the party but to rally behind Vice President Kamala Harris. Had Biden stepped aside in late 2023, there could have been a proper series of Democratic primaries and a new candidate chosen – by real voters – a candidate who would have been both tried and tested in the primaries, and authenticated by the millions of votes they would have received. Of course, that candidate might have been Kamala Harris. But it might not. It's all conjecture. And if not Harris, would that candidate have done any better in November? We just don't know. It's a possible factor, but not the most significant.

Conclusions

As the picture of a Trump victory began to emerge on Election Night, the veteran political commentator Scott Jennings had this to say on CNN:

> I'm interpreting the results tonight as the revenge of the regular old working-class American, the anonymous American who has been crushed, insulted, condescended to. They're not garbage. They're not Nazis. They're just regular people who get up and go to work every day and are trying to make a better life for their kids, and they feel like they have been told to just shut up when they have complained about the things that are hurting them in their own lives.

And veteran Independent/Democratic senator Bernie Sanders, known for his championing of working-class values, came to much the same conclusion. As the dust settled, he praised Kamala Harris for the vigour and focus of her campaign before adding:

> We tried hard to do this – to have a campaign focus or emphasise an economic agenda that speaks to the need of the working class in this country. The status quo is working very well for the people on top, but it's not working well for working people, and the Democratic Party has become far too much a defender of the status quo. You have to acknowledge the pain and the reality of people's lives.

In the end, the key decisive issue of this campaign wasn't abortion or democracy. It was 'affordability' – the way individual Americans thought about their own personal and family finances. It really was 1980 all over again – 'Are you better off than you were four years ago?' And the majority of Americans – just – responded in the negative.

CHAPTER 9

TRUMP, CRIMINAL CASES, THE COURTS AND THE 2024 ELECTION

What you need to know

- An overview of *Bush v Gore* 2000.
- The Supreme Court was not involved in determining the outcome of the November 2024 election.
- Indirectly though, the Supreme Court and state courts, did play an important if secondary role in the lead up to the election and state ballot initiatives.
- The role of the judiciary was particularly important concerning Trump's ability to run largely unconstrained by court proceedings, and in the area of campaign finance.
- The Supreme Court enabled the Democrats to pick up an additional House seat in Alabama, through a 2023 ruling on racial gerrymandering and the 1965 Voting Rights Act.

The context – *Bush v Gore* (2000)

Few political pundits were anticipating the decisive result that November brought, a clear if not emphatic victory for Team MAGA. Even renowned political commentator Larry Sabato in his non-partisan Crystal Ball newsletter, predicted a narrow win for Harris. What was being widely speculated upon was both the likely extreme narrowness of the outcome, and the possibility of the final verdict resting on just a few hundred votes in one or more swing states. With the stakes so high for both sides, a legal challenge going all the way to the Supreme Court seemed not improbable. A repetition of 2000 was feared when the Court awarded victory to Republican candidate, George W. Bush. Back then, the Court by the slimmest of margins, 5-4, reversed the decision of the Florida Supreme Court ordering an immediate manual recount of votes where such recounts had not already taken place. The case was only decided on 12 December, over four weeks after Election Day. At the time inevitably, the decision was viewed as politically partisan, with four conservative justices up against four liberals and swing justice Anthony Kennedy delivering the casting vote. Following the result, Al Gore conceded respectfully if not entirely without some rancour: 'While I strongly disagree with the Court's decision, I accept it.' In the even more febrile and polarised nature of US politics in the 2020s, it is hard to imagine Trump or even Harris responding in quite the same way, let alone their supporters. Fears of civil unrest from the losing side abounded. In the event, thankfully, it did not come to pass. But that still poses the question, what less direct roles did the third branch of US government play in the political proceedings?

Trump – free to campaign

Most presidential candidates in the run-up to the actual presidential campaign are mainly concerned with raising sufficient funds to stay in the race, and securing victory in their party's primaries. Trump's biggest worry were several impending and significant court cases. Writing in *The Guardian* newspaper in November 2024, Sidney Rosenthal summed it up thus,

> 'He understood that his most threatening adversary was the criminal justice system. Trump had to get away with his crimes to survive. The making of the president required the unmaking of justice.'

Rosenthal we should note was a former senior adviser to President Bill Clinton, another US politician who faced some close scrutiny of his private affairs.

Trump had already been convicted by a New York district court back in May 2023 in a civil case for sexual assault against the writer E. Jean Carroll, offences that dated back to the 1990s. The verdict led to Trump having to pay $88.3 million in damages and additionally, considerable legal costs. The decision of the United States District Court for the Southern District of New York and Judge Kaplan did not though weaken his support among his followers. Many indeed echoed his complaints of the trial being no more than a witch hunt by his political opponents. But the Carroll case conviction was far from the only legal case hanging over Trump. He was separately, and again uniquely for a presidential candidate, facing four other criminal cases.

1. **The January 2021 Capitol riots**:This case concerned how far Trump was responsible for inciting the mob that went on to attack the home of the US Congress. This was due to their (mistaken) belief that the 2020 election outcome was false and who demanded that Vice President Pence and the Senate refuse to certify the result. Trump was charged with four criminal counts, including conspiracy to defraud the US and conspiracy against the rights of citizens.

2. **Stormy Daniels and hush money**. The story here was that Trump had illegally falsified business records back in 2016 to use money donated to his political campaign to pay $130,000 to the adult-film actress Stormy Daniels. Ms Daniels was paid the money to keep quiet about her claim that she had sex with Trump, which he has always denied. What was at issue here was not paying the hush money itself, but breaking New York State campaign finance rules which state the purposes to which political donations can be put. Paying off porn actresses with an embarrassing story to tell was not one of them.

3. **Interference in the Georgia presidential election outcome.** Trump and 18 others were accused of criminally conspiring to overturn his very narrow defeat in the state of Georgia in the 2020 election. The investigation, led by Georgia prosecutor Fani Willis, was sparked in part by a leaked phone call in which the former president chillingly asked the state's top election official, Republican Brad Raffensperger, to "find 11,780 votes". It is the iconic photograph of his police mugshot from this case that features on much MAGA merchandise.

4. **Retaining classified documents at his home after leaving the presidency.** The criminal charge involved whether Trump mishandled classified documents by taking them from the White House to his Mar-a-Lago residence after he left office. It was also about whether he obstructed the FBI's efforts to retrieve the files. The majority of the counts fell under the 1917 Espionage Act.

In all four cases, Trump was spared both conviction and sentencing in the vital time period of the election campaign. In some cases, even the hearing itself was postponed/delayed until after November. Had Trump been either sentenced to a jail term or forced to spend many valuable campaign days in court, he might have found campaigning and winning over the small pocket of undecided voters rather harder. How did he manage this political Houdini escape act?

- In the Capitol riots case, no court date had been set by November 2024 in part due to the Supreme Court decision cited below.
- In the hush money case, although found guilty on 34 charges in May 2024, Judge Juan Merchan told Trump's lawyers and prosecutors that he would delay the ruling until 19 November after both defence and prosecutors submitted letters asking for a postponement.
- In the Georgia election case, no date had been set by the time of the election in part due to an effort by Trump and his allies to disqualify the state prosecutor bringing the case, Fani Willis, because of her romantic relationship with a man she hired to work on the case.
- In the classified document case, the case was dismissed by a Florida judge on 15 July, marking a significant legal victory for Trump just days after he survived an assassination attempt in Pennsylvania. As with the Capitol riots case, it may never see the light of day, for largely the same reason namely the Supreme Court immunity case.

Indeed, just after a week or so after the election, Justice Department special counsel Jack Smith announced both his own resignation and that he was ending his two prosecutions of Donald Trump: the Georgia election case and that concerning the retention of classified documents. Neither case as we have seen made it to trial before Trump's election victory which in turn made it impossible for Smith to continue with the charges. Justice Department policy prohibits the prosecution of sitting presidents. In any case, Trump had already vowed to fire Smith within "two seconds" of becoming president again.

Trump v United States 2024

On 1 July 2024 the Supreme Court ruled 6-3 that Trump and presidents more generally had "absolute immunity" from charges for acts that fell under their "core constitutional powers" like appointing officials and "presumptive immunity" for official acts taken while in office but were not immune from acts that are not part of their official duties. The court decided the case along predicable partisan lines, with six conservative justices on one side and three liberal justices on the other. The liberal view was summed up by Justice Sotomayor who wrote in her dissent that the ruling "makes a mockery of the principle, foundational to our Constitution and system of Government, that no man is above the law," Trump himself was delighted, calling it on his social media website, Truth Social, "BIG WIN FOR OUR CONSTITUTION AND DEMOCRACY."

This decision at the very least delayed the ongoing cases against him, kicking the can further down the alley. With hindsight, might this case assume a similar importance to *Bush v Gore* representing a pivotal moment when the courts dabbled directly in presidential politics. On both occasions furthermore, a Republican candidate 'struck lucky' with the court's composition at the time. What was different in 2024, is that it might well have consequences for how Trump behaves in office knowing he had been granted a high degree of immunity. Only history will tell if Sotomayor was being unduly alarmist or alarmingly prophetic.

In summary, despite multiple legal cases and even a couple of convictions, Trump was largely given a free pass to pursue his third presidential campaign. It is a moot point whether this represents a collective failure by the courts to check the power even of an ex-president as he was at the time, or whether as Trump himself phrased it, "The real verdict is going to be [on] 5 November, by the people." The people's jury on that count at any rate acquitted Mr Trump.

Campaign finance, the FEC and 2024

Amid all the focus on the legal issues surrounding Trump, it would be all too easy to overlook another, much less high profile development, that has played into this election. This revolves around campaign finance. Ever since the 2010 landmark case *Citizens United*, SuperPACs have become major players in campaign finance and thus the whole election campaign. Simply put, they enable unlimited sums to be spent independently of candidates' own campaigns, on supporting or opposing candidates running for office. Furthermore, there are ways for donors to remain secret if they choose. All donations to candidates' own campaigns are capped and large donors' identity made public, and SuperPAC spending must be declared to the Federal Election Commission (FEC). However, 501(c) groups may make donations to SuperPACs and not reveal who is behind these donations. One example in 2024 was Bill Gates. Unlike many fellow Silicon Valley megadonors, he wanted to keep his $50m donation to Kamala Harris low key. He therefore made it via a 501(c) group to Future Forward a leading SuperPAC supporting her candidacy.

'Red-boxing'

Alongside this huge explosion in 'dark money' whose origins cannot easily be traced, there has been a continued dilution of rules concerning campaign finance. In 2024 it was revealed that the FEC itself was turning a blind eye to coordination between the official campaigns of candidates and outside groups including SuperPACs. This included a tactic or loophole known as 'red-boxing'. Essentially, candidate campaigns leave a directive to groups on their public-facing websites describing the kind of targeted advertising that they want, which outside spending groups then use to craft advertisements on their behalf. An apparent breach of the separation required under existing laws. One study found that 240 candidates, from both parties, used this tactic in the 2022 mid-terms. Why the term 'red-boxing'? Around the text on many campaign websites is a literal red box – flagging committees to pay attention and giving them enough information/ sound bites to create their own political ads.

Joint fundraising committees

Here we enter another niche area of that complex topic of campaign finance. A "joint fundraising committee" (JFC) is a body that supposedly exists purely to raise money for its participants, which could include candidates' own campaigns, political party committees, leadership PACs, and super PACs. Under the Federal Election Campaign Act (FECA), JFCs exist "solely" to raise funds for their participants — not to engage directly in what is termed in candidate advocacy. Nevertheless, in an advisory opinion request issued in early October 2024, the FEC agreed that JFCs could pay for an ad that primarily advocated for candidates rather than raised issues or simply funnelled money to other groups.

The net result of these two developments? The 2024 election would prove even costlier than that of 2020, when all the races from the presidency downwards are taken into account. So, there was no landmark ruling concerning how campaign finance should be regulated. But nonetheless, exploitation and in the case of the FEC, acquiescence with, existing loopholes in the law and previous court decisions, ensured that the First Amendment would provide cover for billionaire mega donors and wealthy corporations to ply their trade of buying political influence. Unlike the legal challenges to Trump, this situation attracted a more bipartisan degree of support. Both parties after all, have their billionaire backers. What price democracy indeed!

State courts and abortion initiatives

If campaign finance is a tricky topic to understand fully, abortion seems a lot more straightforward to comprehend. The basic position currently would appear to be:

1. Abortion following the *Dobbs v Jackson* case that infamously/famously, depending on one's standpoint, overturned *Roe v Wade*, abortion is an issue to be decided at state level. A federal abortion law favouring either side, pro-choice or pro-life, looks extremely unlikely not least due to the need for 60 Senate votes.

2. The way forward and the new battleground would therefore be via state legislatures and/or ballot initiatives. Many states have already engaged in this process with the majority to date favouring a degree of protection for abortion rights.

That though is something of a simplification. Particularly in red states where Republicans control the state government, it often proved a struggle even to get a pro-choice initiative on to the November ballot. Missouri offers one such example.

- Initially, two state lawmakers joined private anti-abortion plaintiffs to challenge the initiative as insufficiently detailed. Just days before the deadline for printing ballots in August, a trial judge ordered the initiative removed from the November ballot.

- Although the judge paused their decision pending appeal, Missouri Secretary of State, Jay Ashcroft, removed the constitutional pro-choice amendment himself.

- The Missouri Supreme Court then overruled his decision, allowing the proposed amendment to appear on the ballot just hours before ballots had to be printed.

A reminder if nothing else, that the courts have an influence on American politics beyond helping to determine the presidency or the financial aspects of elections.

And finally... how the US Supreme Court delivered an extra House seat to Democrats in Alabama

2024 was also notable for how a Supreme Court decision can be both unexpected and influence the composition of the House of Representatives. It all boils down to the 1965 Voting Rights Act and gerrymandering – the process of drawing House district lines for partisan political advantage, a tactic used by both parties across the states where the state legislature controls redistricting. Congressional redistricting occurs every ten years after the national census.

In summary the story up to 2023 went as follows:
- The Voting Rights Act 1965 (VRA) among other clauses, forbade the negative use of a race based gerrymander. In other words, under Section 2 redistricting could not deliberately exclude a racial minority from 'electing representatives of their choice', for example by splitting or 'cracking' their voters across several districts that had white majorities. It was permissible though to 'pack' a minority vote i.e. concentrate Black or Hispanic voters into districts to give them a very good opportunity to elect someone from their own racial group. These are termed 'majority minority districts'.

- The VRA was though significantly weakened in 2013 by the decision in *Shelby v Holder* which gutted Section 5 requiring federal preclearance (approval) of redistricting in certain counties with a poor record of racial discrimination. This was seen at the time as a reflection of the conservative drift of the court.

- Another 2013 case, *Raucho v Common Cause*, found that political gerrymandering per se was not unconstitutional.
- Alabama, a deep red southern state had traditionally comprised seven House districts. Six majority white (and all safely Republican), and one majority minority district (safely Democrat).

So, what changed in 2023? Firstly, the Republican dominated state legislature redrew congressional districts in 2021 preserving the 6-1 split above and the map was approved by the state's Republican governor in November. They achieved this by continuing to 'crack' the Black vote between the 2nd and 3rd Districts. However, Alabama's black population had grown slightly to 27% yet this proposed map would only 'give' them 1/7 (14%) of the districts. Legal challenges ensured: a federal district court struck down the new map, but the Supreme Court pressed the pause button on the district court's decision saying it was too close to the 2022 mid-terms. The 2022 congressional elections were thus allowed to proceed with an apparently illegal electoral map.

Come 2023, the whole issue went before the Supreme Court which delivered its surprise 5-4 verdict in *Allen v Milligan*, that upheld the earlier district court ruling. Surprising because the Court with its 6-3 conservative majority was widely expected to gut Section 2 as it had Section 5 in the *Shelby* case. Two conservative justices, Chief Justice Roberts and Justice Kavanaugh, sided with the three liberal justices. Alabama Republicans tried one last trick. They slightly re-drew their original map to increase the black vote in a second district but keeping it at around 40%, some distance short of giving Democrats a decent chance of winning the seat. This revised map was also struck down in the courts, and the result was that the district court appointed a special master to redraw the electoral map thereby taking it out of the hands of the state government. It was this new map on which the November 2024 election was fought, and the result: the Democrats gained two instead of one House seats. The table below shows how the racial gerrymander in the original 2021 map was overturned in the final court approved map used in 2024.

Table 9.1 How Allen v Milligan changed Alabama's congressional map

House District	Black voter percentage old map	Black voter percentage new map
1st	25%	15%
2nd	29%	47%
3rd	24%	25%
4th	7%	6%
5th	18%	17%
6th	19%	17%
7th	54%	51%

(Figures from the Princeton Gerrymandering project)

The takeaways from this little saga?

- Federal law and Supreme Court rulings can overrule individual states.
- States in the end have to comply with court decisions.
- Race and voting remain closely aligned especially in the Deep South.
- Court decisions can directly affect election outcomes.
- Supreme Court decisions can be unpredictable.

Conclusion

While the courts may not in the end have been called upon to tilt the scales of justice in either a red or blue direction, they were not entirely on the political touchline in 2024. A timely reminder if needed, that US elections in some ways often involve all three branches of government.

CHAPTER 10
INTEREST GROUPS AND THE 2024 ELECTION

What you need to know
- The role traditionally played by interest groups in US elections.
- Changes and continuities apparent in their roles and stances in 2024.
- An assessment of the overall political influence exercised by interest groups.

The traditional functions of interest groups in US elections

Interest groups (also known as pressure groups) are a long-established part of the political backdrop against which US elections occur. Given the size and diversity of the United States, there are thousands of groups vying for influence with both lawmakers and executive agencies. Many represent national issues including social issues such as abortion or gay rights, while others represent specific policy issues such as gun rights or the environment. Some, meanwhile, seek to represent a particular group of voters sharing a common profile. This could include those with disabilities, workers from various sectors represented by trade unions (more commonly termed organised labour in the US), or employer/business groups such as the US Chamber of Commerce. Around election time, these groups rev into action seeking policy pledges from candidates that align with their own, getting actively involved in campaigns.

Frequently used tactics during election campaigns include:
- **Issuing scorecards or voting guides** for their supporters. These will often rate candidates on a scale of A to F. The National Rifle Association (NRA) and NORML, a group that has been advocating for the legalisation of marijuana since the 1970s, are two such examples.
- **Offering endorsements** to candidates based on their voting record, or if not an incumbent, their previous actions or public statements. These commonly appear on candidates' websites.

- **Donating money** either directly to candidates' own campaigns, or to a SuperPAC supporting them. Note that interest groups have their own PACs from which they make political donations or spend money on political activities.

- **Running issue-based ads** that either support their favoured candidate, or and often more common, attacking their opponent. Such ads focus on how far a candidate supports the group's chosen stance on issues. An NRA ad for example will focus on whether or not a candidate is a 'friend' of the Second Amendment.

Traditional interest group alignments

It probably comes as little surprise that groups often endorse candidates of the same party, in every election cycle. This very much aligns with the policy stances taken by candidates which in turn reflect, usually, those of the national party. America being America though, these matters are not always so straightforward. Some candidates receive endorsements from perhaps unexpected quarters, while some interest groups take a more bipartisan approach to election campaigns, preferring above all to back likely winners rather than adopt a highly partisan stance. That has traditionally been the case with the National Association of Realtors (estate agents) who routinely end up making political donations via their PAC on an almost 50/50 basis between candidates from each party. Nonetheless we can make some generally accurate labelling when it comes to which party certain groups usually line up behind.

Table 10.1 Examples of Democrat-leaning and Republican-leaning interest groups

Democrat-backing groups	Republican-backing groups
Pro-choice groups: e.g. Reproductive Freedom for All (previously NARAL Pro-Choice America)	Pro-life groups: e.g. Susan B. Anthony List
LGBTQ+ groups: e.g. Human Rights Campaign	Evangelical Christian groups advocating for religious liberty and opposition to an expansion of LGBTQ+ rights: e.g. Family Research Council

Gun control groups: e.g. Everytown for Gun Safety	Groups defending Second amendment rights: e.g. National Rifle Association (NRA)
Environmental groups: e.g. League of Conservation Voters	Certain business sectors especially the oil and coal sectors: e.g. American Petroleum Institute
Organised labour: e.g. AFL-CIO	Some police unions: e.g. Fraternal Order of Police
Legalisation of soft drugs: e.g. NORML	Groups advocating for small government, tax cuts and greater deregulation for businesses: e.g. Club for Growth

Unsurprisingly, as the table above shows, in large measure endorsements followed a predictable pattern. Table 10.2 takes as an example the highly competitive Senate race in Arizona.

Table 10.2 The Gallego-Lake Senate race in Arizona, 2024

Ruben Gallego (Democrat) – winner	Kari Lake (Republican) – defeated
• Planned Parenthood Action Fund • Giffords (a pro-gun control group) • VoteVets (military veterans not animal doctors!) • Arizona Police Association* • League of Conservation Voters • Human Rights Campaign (a pro LGBTQ+ rights group) • End Citizens United/Let America Vote • Jewish Democratic Council of America	• National Rifle Association – Political Victory Fund • Club for Growth (a business group favouring free enterprise and a smaller state) • Oil & Gas Workers Association • Republican National Hispanic Assembly • Arizona Conference of Police and Sheriffs (AZCOPS)* • Arizona Fraternal Order of Police • Republican Jewish Coalition

Note: In Arizona as elsewhere, police unions may not always back a single party or candidate. In Arizona, different law enforcement groups backed different candidates.

But politics would not really be politics if matters weren't a little more complex than this simple binary divide between Democrats and Republicans when it comes to interest groups.

Changes and developments in 2024

The rough alignments and allegiances of interest groups remain pretty consistent across election cycles. For example, feminist groups such as EMILYs List are very unlikely to suddenly switch from backing female Democrat candidates to supporting Republicans. However, three discernible shifts can be identified, all relevant to the 2024 election.

- Groups can lose influence within its chosen party and political orbit due to broader cultural and political trends.
- A group through its own actions and mistakes can become weaker both financially and politically.
- Occasionally groups might subtly shift their allegiance due to pressure and feedback from members.

The following case studies illustrate each point.

Case study 1: The Family Research Council (FRC)

The FRC is an evangelical Christian group advocating on a number of social issues from a conservative biblical perspective. Among these key issues are abortion and defending religious freedom and its place in public life, such as allowing private Christian schools to be eligible for publicly-funded education vouchers and protecting children from what they would term dangerous gender critical views in classrooms. The FRC's core values align closely with much of the conservative Republican agenda, what is often termed the 'religious right'.

But they faced a dilemma in 2024. Trump while courting (and winning) the white evangelical vote, is a convicted felon, with a blemished record when it comes to his attitudes towards women. In addition, while the appointment in his first term of three conservative Supreme Court justices led to the overturning of *Roe v Wade*, he showed no appetite for supporting a federal abortion ban. He preferred instead to leave the abortion issue to individual states. Abortion restrictions are politically toxic for the Republicans in many states including those that are reliably red. Furthermore, America as a whole is becoming more secular and less religious. For a group like the FRC, it was a case in 2024 of being somewhere between a rock and a hard place. The statement below published on their website summed up well this 'lesser of two evils' dilemma.

'It has always been my view that evangelical Christians should never feel completely at home in either party, and this sentiment is especially relevant in 2024. However, as long as Democrats continue on their current trajectory and persist in pursuing radical policies regarding life, marriage, and religious freedom, I suspect that most conservative Christians will continue supporting Republican candidates, if for no other reason than to blunt the leftward lurch of the Democratic Party.' (David Closson, a senior FRC official)

The not so subtly coded message? Republicans, especially Trump, may be far from perfect, but the Democrats are an existential threat. Not a ringing endorsement of Team MAGA then.

Case study 2: The National Rifle Association (NRA)

At its peak, the NRA was one of the most powerful advocacy groups in the Republican 'politico-sphere'. An A+ rating from the group was a 'must have' for pretty much every Republican candidate. But times have changed.

1. Mass shootings, not least in schools and places of worship, have made many Americans more receptive to greater gun controls such as automatic background checks and making it easier for law enforcement to take away the guns of those with a history of mental illness. While even Harris and Walz were not shy to acknowledge their own gun ownership credentials, a small handgun for self- defence in Harris' case, the more absolutist stance of the NRA against moderate gun control measures has fewer takers.

2. As an organisation, the NRA has been through a period of prolonged turmoil. Its long-standing CEO, Wayne LaPierre, was found guilty by a New York court in February 2024 of misspending millions of dollars of the group's money on private flights, vacations and other lavish perks. He was ordered to pay over $4.3 million in compensation to the group. It was reported that

3. LaPierre had spent over $11 million on private jets alone. But this was not the only problem facing the group. It had earlier reported a $36 million deficit in 2018 and, in 2021, had unsuccessfully filed for bankruptcy and tried to move its headquarters from New York to Texas. Its declining finances and membership posed significant problems.

These self-inflicted wounds and a shifting public mood meant that it was a much diminished organisation by 2024. Having dispensed around $29 million in direct campaign contributions and independent expenditure in 2020, it could only muster around $11 million in 2024. A lot of that expenditure was focused on two especially tight Senate races in Ohio and Montana. Interestingly, only 63% Republican candidates (71% 2022 midterms) received an 'A' rating from the NRA. Nearly all the remainder received a '?' suggesting that the group could be on the path dreaded by all interest group, that of perceived irrelevance.

Case study 3: The Teamsters Union

The Teamsters are a major player in organised labour in the US. They enjoy particularly high membership in the haulage industry. With over 1.3 million members nowadays, they represent a wide range of workers across the country. As their website boasts, they count as members, 'vegetable workers in California; sanitation workers in New York; brewers in St. Louis; newspaper workers in Seattle; construction workers in Las Vegas; zookeepers in Pennsylvania; health care workers in Rhode Island.' A union movement like the Teamsters was traditionally associated with the Democrats, and an emphasis on standing up for ordinary working people going back to FDR and the New Deal of the 1930s. In 2020 they backed the Biden–Harris ticket.

But 2024 was different. Firstly, its president, Sean O'Brien, spoke at both the Republican and Democratic national conventions, the first ever Teamster president to have a prime-time speaking slot at the Republican event. Secondly, in another break with the past, the union refused to endorse either candidate. Its subsequent press release stated,

> 'President Joe Biden won the support of Teamsters voting in straw polls at local unions between April–July prior to his exit from the race.
>
> But in independent electronic and phone polling from July–September, a majority of voting members twice selected Trump for a possible Teamsters endorsement over Harris. The union's extensive member polling showed no majority support for Vice President Harris and no universal support among the membership for President Trump.'

Again, the shorthand version was our membership was divided, neither candidate is ideal, so members can make their own choice. Perhaps it also reflects Trump's appeal among many blue-collar workers.

Another dimension of interest group activity to consider with the 2024 election is that of the endorsement of candidates from across the political divide. From time to time, we can see groups which largely endorse candidates from just one particular party, back the occasional candidate from the other party. Although 87% of Democrat candidates scored an 'F' from the NRA in 2024, Alaska's sole House member, Democrat Mary Peltola, received an 'A'. Arguably though it did her little good as she narrowly lost to Mark Begich, her Republican challenger. Contrastingly, NORML usually back Democrat candidates, who are largely more inclined to be open to the relaxation of laws concerning soft drugs, influenced in part perhaps by the racial dimension to convictions for drug use which disproportionately affect non-white Americans. But among all the Californian Democratic House candidates backed by NORML in 2024 was also a lone Republican, Tom McClintock who represents the 5th District, whose voting record recorded a more libertarian approach to recreational and medicinal soft drug use. These two examples show that not all candidates necessarily fall into line with all their fellow party members. US politics retains an element of the local and the personal alongside the national trend towards polarisation and uniformity.

Putting the perspective into interest groups

One thing though that 2024 arguably suggests with interest groups, is that their influence in US politics is declining. Yes, a long established and undoubtedly important player in the progressive political corner such as EMILYs List could raise and spend $57 million. But set this alongside the growing prominence of billionaire donors. In 2024 this list was topped by the world's richest man, Elon Musk who contributed a jaw-breaking $277 million to Republican causes in the 2024 cycle, – around $243 million was via his own Great America PAC. One estimate was that the tech sector alone contributed around $273 million to Trump and $121 million to Harris. The role of interest groups in bankrolling or influencing election outcomes has become increasingly challenged. As we saw in Chapter 4, it was not the misgiving of key interest groups in the Democrat orbit that led Biden to pull his candidacy. Rather, it was the reluctance of megadonors to whip out their chequebooks. Perhaps we should ask less whether it is interest groups that undermine aspects of US democracy, and more whether it is the danger posed by America's billionaire elite. A bipartisan problem certainly, but will it yield a bipartisan solution?

STUDENT QUESTIONS

These questions can be used as a helpful way to make notes on the major points of each chapter.

Chapter 1 – The Invisible Primary

1. Analyse the data presented in Table 1.1.
2. Who were the three people who challenged President Biden in the Democrat's nomination race? Comment on their relative importance.
3. What were the major changes proposed by Democratic National Committee regarding the 2024 presidential primaries? What was their purpose? To what extent were they implemented?
4. Who were President Trump's main opponents in the 2024 Republican nomination race?
5. What effect did the series of the five intra-party debates have on the race?
6. Why did President Trump not participate in these debates?

Chapter 2 – The Primaries

1. What was significant about the result of the Republican caucuses in Iowa on 15 January?
2. What three reasons are suggested why President Trump triumphed quite easily in the 2024 Republican primaries?
3. How serious an intra-party challenge did President Biden face in the Democratic primaries in 2024?
4. Analyse the data presented in Figure 2.1.
5. To what extent have caucuses declined in importance in each party in recent decades?
6. By analysing the data in Table 2.3, explain frontloading in 2024 and the effect it had on the nomination race in each party.

Chapter 3 – The Biden–Trump Debate

1. What four things were new/different about the Biden–Trump debate?
2. Analyse the data in Figure 3.1.
3. What was Biden's main problem in this debate?
4. Summarise Amy Walter's comment in Box 3.1.
5. What is 'bounce'? What happened regarding 'bounce' after this debate?
6. What was ironic about the effect of this debate on President Biden?

Chapter 4 – Biden's Exit

1. Why did Biden's position appear strong at the start of 2024?
2. How pivotal in his withdrawal from the race was the televised debate?
3. Why do you think Biden did not quit the race earlier?
4. How significant was Biden catching Covid in influencing the final outcome?
5. Why was the opinion of major donors so important?
6. Do you regard those who plotted his downfall as traitors or heroes from the perspective of the Democratic party?

Chapter 5 – Selecting a Running Mate

1. What do you think the 'Power' comment from VEEP suggests about the traditional perceptions of the role of vice president?
2. Why was 2024 unusual when it came to the selection of VP candidates?
3. What is meant by the term 'second stage of the rocket' and 'balancing the ticket' when it comes to selecting vice presidential candidates?
4. What were some of the weaknesses of the other candidates under consideration for the VP position?
5. There are a number of factors put forward as to why Vance and Walz were eventually chosen. Which two in each case do you think were the most important?

Chapter 6 – The Party Conventions

1. What is the difference between the traditional role performed by conventions and their role in the current political calendar of presidential election years?
2. What factors influence the choice of location for conventions?
3. What potentially divisive topics did each party want to keep off the convention floor?
4. What were some of the key features in the party platforms of each party?
5. What factors explain Harris' pick of Walz as her running mate?
6. Why could both conventions be seen as a success for their respective parties?

Chapter 7 – The General Election Campaign

1. What was the state of the race at the start of September?
2. Analyse the data in Table 7.2.
3. Summarise the significance of the Harris–Trump TV debate.
4. Analyse the data in Figure 7.1.
5. From Table 7.5, choose five individual policies on which Harris and Trump clearly disagreed.
6. Analyse the data in Table 7.6.

Chapter 8 – Who Won, and Why

1. What six reasons does the author give for why Trump won?
2. Analyse the data in Table 8.1 and Figures 8.1 and 8.2.
3. Summarise the data in Table 8.2 and Megan McArdle's comments in Box 8.1.
4. According to Fareed Zakaria, what was 'the first big error' of the Biden administration?
5. Why was Harris' comment on 'The View' about her links to Joe Biden problematic?
6. Why did the accusation that Harris was 'too leftwing' resonate with many voters?

7. Why did Latino voters swing so strongly to Trump?

8. Analyse the data in Figure 8.3 and explain the 2024 figure.

9. Why did Trump do so much better than 2020 amongst Black men?

10. How important were young voters in the swing states?

11. Why did non-college-educated voters support Trump in such large numbers?

12. Analyse the data in Table 8.5.

13. How important was Biden's late exit to the result of the election?

14. Summarise the comments made by Scott Jennings and Bernie Sanders.

Chapter 9 – Trump, criminal cases, the courts and the 2024 election

1. What happened in *Bush v Gore*?

2. Why was it widely believed that the Supreme Court might get involved in the 2024 election?

3. What were the five charges/court cases over which Trump faced prosecution in the lead up to the election?

4. How and why did the ruling in *Trump v United States* help Trump's campaign?

5. What happened to two of Trump's court cases after he won the November election?

6. What in theory must not occur between a candidate's own campaign and a SuperPAC?

7. What is 'red-boxing' and why is it controversial?

8. What is a JFC?

9. How did the FEC arguably further weaken campaign finance rules?

10. Does the Missouri example support or weaken the argument that the courts help uphold democracy?

11. What did *Allen v Mulligan* decide about Alabama's redistricting?

12. How could you apply the Alabama redistricting saga to other A-level Politics topics beyond the Supreme court?

Chapter 10 – Interest Groups and the 2024 Election

1. In what ways can interest groups in the US get involved in election campaigns?

2. Looking at the table of typical left/right leaning groups, how and why do you think this has come about in the case of the groups listed?

3. Why did evangelical Christian groups face something of a dilemma at the 2024 election?

4. Why was the NRA much weaker going into the 2024 election?

5. What is the greatest fear for any interest group?

6. Why did the Teamsters not back either main candidate in 2024?

7. Who was the largest single donor in the 2024 campaign?

8. What is the evidence that interest groups are perhaps losing ground in terms of overall political influence?

Printed in Great Britain
by Amazon

57893878R00064